# A HAVEN IN HELL

Cameos of the Western Front

# A Haven in Hell

Talbot House, Poperinghe

PAUL CHAPMAN

Edited by
Ted Smith

with an introduction by
Tony Spagnoly

First published in Great Britain 2000
by Pen & Sword Books Limited

Published in Large Print 2001 by ISIS Publishing Ltd.
7 Centremead, Osney Mead, Oxford OX2 0ES
by arrangement with Pen & Sword Books Limited

**British Library Cataloguing in Publication Data**
Chapman, Paul
A haven in hell. – Large print ed.
1. Clayton, Tubby
2. Talbot House – History
3. Talbot House
4. Large type books
5. World War, 1914–1918 – Western Front
6. World War, 1914–1918 – Social aspects – Belgium – Poperinghe
I. Title
II. Smith, Ted, 1936–
940.4′779493

ISBN 0–7531–5613–X (hb)
ISBN 0–7531–5614–8 (pb)

Printed and bound by Antony Rowe, Chippenham and Reading

# DEDICATION

To Jacques Ryckebosch.

To my friend Gladys Lunn for giving me the reason to return and for having faith in me.

To Ann Clayton for her inspiration.

To my Mother, Father, wife Sandra and daughter Angela.

To All the Elder Brethren.

# CONTENTS

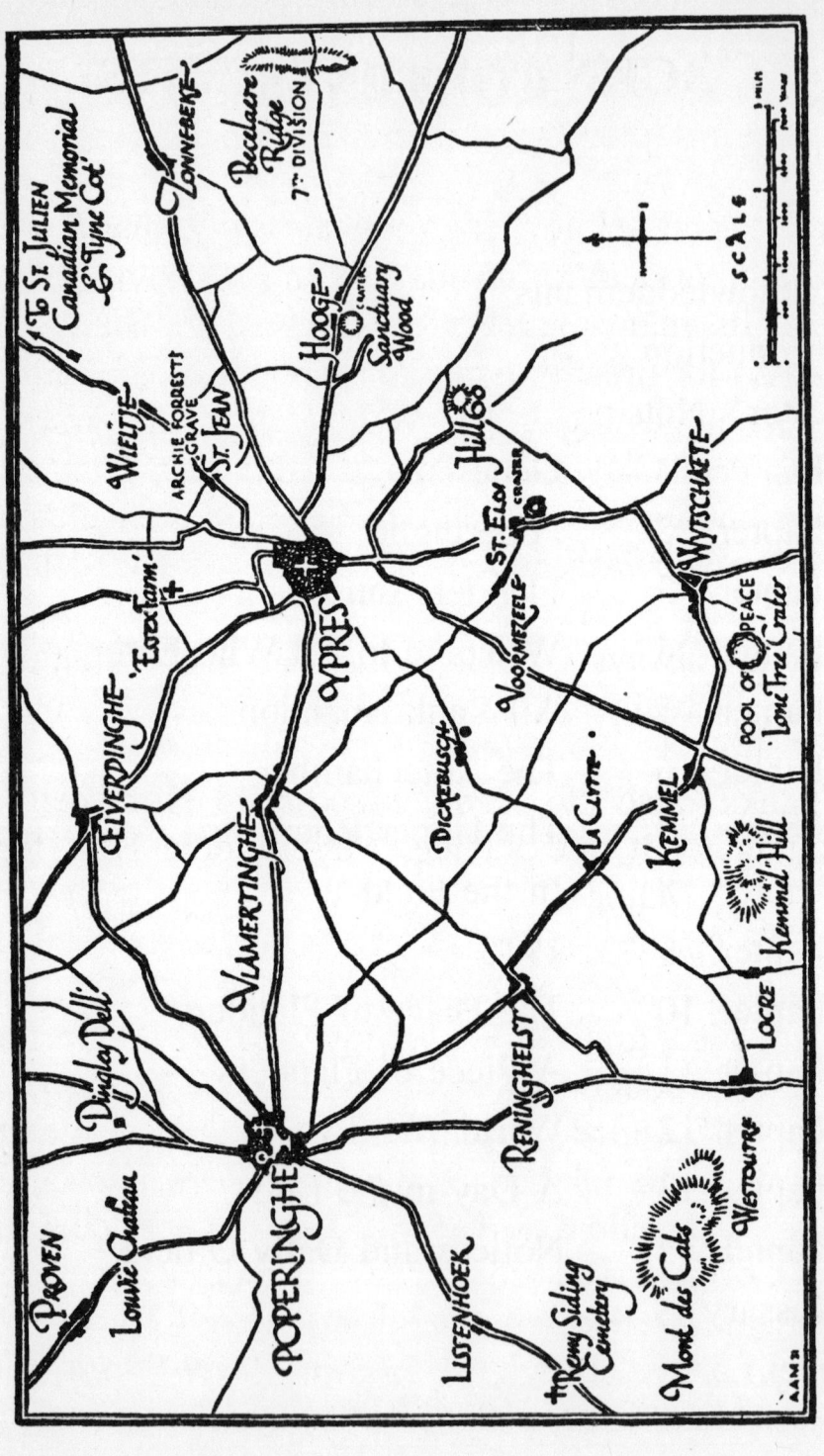

# ACKNOWLEDGEMENTS

I realise, and acknowledge unreservedly, that this book owes a great deal to the support and assistance of many others. Its many pages are dedicated to Gladys Lunn (SSAFA) for breathing countless hours of life into them and for suggesting *A Haven In Hell* in the first place. And to Ann Clayton (author of *Chavasse, Double VC*) for her enthusiastic support and encouragement.

I am particularly indebted to my good friend Jacques Ryckebosch for his support, unstinting help with my research, always keeping me on the straight and narrow factually, and continuous updating through to completion.

Thanks also to Lyn Macdonald for her kind encouragement and advice, Major Tonie Holt for his assistance, Major Lake (Royal Welch Fusiliers) for *The War The Infantry Knew* and Lady Lever for *Clayton of Toc H.*

I am also grateful to Wendy Attreed, Peter Barton (Parapet Productions), Jean Battheu (Belgium), John Biggerstaff, Lance Corporal Stuart Bingley (Coldstream Guards), Gino Clabau (Belgium), Steve Clews, Rose Coates, Gabrielle Coevoet van Landschoote (Belgium), Noel Cornick, Russell Davies, Canon Peter Delaney, Christiaan DePoorter (Belgium), John Dray, Arlette Duclos Lahaye (Belgium), Martin Marix-Evans, Martin Fryatt, Alice Greer, Mark Hemsley, Dr. John Laffin,

Mike Lyddiard, Brian Little, Jan Louagie (Belgium), Dr. Alf Peacock, Ruth Prince, George Sutherland (Belgium), Julian Sykes and Dennis Till.

And finally two people to whom I owe my undying gratitude and deepest admiration — Ted Smith, my Editor, without whose enthusiasm, design and photography, this book would never have seen the light of day, and Tony Spagnoly for his encouragement, many kindnesses and Introduction.

At the time of going to press the literary executors of certain authors have not been traced and the author will be grateful for any information as to their identity and whereabouts.

# INTRODUCTION

In "Plain Tales from Flanders" published in 1930 and written by the Reverend "Tubby" Clayton, the founder of the "Toc H" brotherhood of faith and friendship, a leading chapter is entitled "The House that love built" and that heading still seems to sum up exactly what "Toc H" still stands for!

The Great War period of 1914–1918 is still prominent in our memory and national consciousness as a time of national loss, sacrifice and suffering, and yet amidst the savagery and brutality of battle, stood moments of hope and nobility like beacons! The conception and foundation of Toc H by the Reverend Phillip Byard Clayton was one such enlightened moment. He founded "Toc H" in 1922 to maintain the camaraderie of the trenches as he saw it!

It is always a pleasure to read a new "labour of love" written from close to the heart as Paul Chapman's fresh look at the "Toc H" tale "A Haven in Hell", so therefore to be asked to pen a short introduction is indeed a pleasure!

I have known Paul for a long period, and his deep abiding interest and support for the "Toc H" organisation, so his plans to cast new light on an old story were valid in my opinion as the famous world-wide brotherhood was in need of a modern appraisal. In Ted Smith he has been lucky enough to find an editor who recognised immediately the potential of his proposed work.

The title symbolises the "Old House" first rented by Tubby Clayton in late 1915, together with his friend the Rev. Neville Talbot, a senior chaplain with the 6th division then serving in the Ypres Salient.

The history of "Toc H" had modest beginnings in the mud of Flanders. The house, purchased in Poperinghe was almost named "Church House" — a place to provide weary spirits with short periods of rest and recuperation quickly became "Talbot House" serving as a poignant memorial in tribute to the memory of Lt Gilbert Talbot, brother of Neville; both sons of a leading Anglican Bishop! Gilbert had fallen in the summer fighting of 1915 around Hooge Château near Ypres, and his grave can now be found today at Sanctuary Wood Cemetery near the famed Menin Road, Ypres. Tubby Clayton incorporated the name around army signals language of the time, and "Toc H" entered the records for all posterity.

The house stands proudly at 43, Gasthuisstraat just off the main square in Poperinghe, and the original "Every Man's Club" board can be clearly seen by all. Poperinghe was then a small town to the west of the Ypres Salient and generally out of enemy shell range until the last eighteen months of the war. The town was used very much by British troops for rest periods when out of the front line at Ypres. It would become an "Oasis of peace and tranquillity" for the many young men seeking calm, away from the uproar and danger of battle! Here, weary and frightened they could recover in a spiritual way, or indulge in lively debate — something the more intellectually active might have missed in the trenches?

It was from this simple idea that the worldwide fraternity with its adopted symbol of an early Christian lamp of peace has flowered like an acorn, and Paul Chapman with fluent clarity delivers the modern message that Tubby Clayton would have been proud of. And this is the association we have come to admire and respect through the years. He could never have realised as he once dodged shells along the rail banks at "Transport Farm" Zillebeke taking the sacraments to waiting soldiers, that the ideals he was proposing in the midst of war would blaze a message of hope and faith not only for the rest of the conflict, but shine like a beacon well beyond that to our own more sophisticated times.

We, in our turn would also be drawn to the "Old House" and all it represented in ever increasing numbers. We too, like the lonely soldier of yesteryear would seek within ourselves that simple message he left us back in 1915. To share that calm reflective atmosphere of those quiet corners and rooms so very evocative of the many thousands who once found sanctuary there.

To stroll at peace in that quiet English type garden at the rear of the house which must have reminded so many homesick lads of what they had left behind? and finally to seek the "culmination" of every visit to Talbot House when we climbed the stairs to the "Upper Room" still retaining that unique spirit of sacrifice and duty left behind by the many thousands of young men who had passed this way in another age, never returned home, and now lay in their warrior graves all over the old "Salient". Yes, the "Upper Room" still has that intangible magic, and the founder would himself rest easy to know his vision has evolved in such a way that inspires sincere works as Paul has produced in these modern times!

He has captured the prevailing spirit of Talbot House and "Toc H" with "Haven", and his readership should entail success for a job well done. A place where the muddy frightened young soldier could grasp the realities of "another world", that short restful interlude for a weary inner self if only for a brief few joyous hours.

Paul Chapman with this "Haven" certainly perpetuates a noble inspiration which will endure!

Tony Spagnoly, May 2000

# EDITOR'S NOTE

Talbot House, Every Man's Club, 1915–?, Poperinghe is probably known by all enthusiasts of the old Western Front of the Great War, and is a place that thousands have visited, with many having taken the opportunity to spend a night or nights there. All know its reason for being, but few know of the conception of Every Man's Club, its activities and progress during the war years, the birth of the Toc H movement and its development in the post war years, the acquisition of the house itself, its survival and upkeep in the Second World War or its progress to the end of the twentieth century.

Today, Talbot House is a living museum where visitors are treated in exactly the same way as those who passed through its doors during the Great War years. A friendly greeting and the offer of a cup of tea on arrival, a house rule established by Tubby Clayton in 1915, is still the order of the day; a room for the night, or as many nights as is needed is still on offer; the fully equipped kitchen is there for all to use on a self-catering basis; the lounge and reading room serve the same function as they did, and the garden is for the use of visitors in exactly the way it was between 1915 and 1918. Much of the furnishing is exactly as it was, and many of the notices posted by Tubby Clayton and the artifacts collected during the war are there, in place. The paintings and illustrations donated by many of the soldiers still hang on the walls and, of course, the crowning feature, the Chapel in the Upper Room, is still there to see for those who are prepared to risk the steep climb up Jacob's Ladder as did those thousands of soldiers between 1915 and 1918, 25,000 of them alone taking Holy Communion there. Tubby Clayton had a vision and worked for most of his life to realise it. Nothing reflects better his aspiration than the incomplete date-span, "1915–?" on the hanging sign above the doors of Talbot House.

Paul Chapman has brought to the reader the history of the house and its contents, and brings to life the multitude of events that took place in and around it as well as telling the little known stories of Tubby Clayton's frequent trips to the front line to minister to the men in the trenches around Ypres. To those regular visitors, and those yet to visit Talbot House, this book will be of great interest, offering insight and understanding of what a few men with spirit, belief, faith and tenacious will-power can bring to thousands of others suffering indescribable privations and hardship, both physically and spiritually.

Ted Smith, May 2000

# CHAPTER
# ONE

# Genesis

Suddenly, as if lightened,
An unwonted splendour brightened
And he saw the Blessed Vision
Of our Lord
*Henry Wadsworth Longfellow*

Philip Thomas Byard Clayton was born in Queensland, Australia on Saturday, 12th December 1885, the sixth child of Isobel Sheppard and Reginald Clayton, who ran a sheep farm and sugar plantation. The family returned to England in 1887 where Reginald formed a business in the import and export of Australian and New Zealand goods. As a boy Philip spent most of his spare time exploring London whilst attending Colet Court and St. Paul's school in the City. During his time here he became known as "PBC" and, due to his rotund stature, "Tubby". In this respect he was called "Tubby Junior" as his uncle, the vicar of St. Mary Magdalene, a man of colossal proportions and more deserving of the title, was already known as Tubby Clayton. Tubby "Junior" was often seen walking, deep in discussion on some obscure topic, with the High Master, F. W. Walker, a man feared

1

and revered by the other masters and scholars alike. Young Tubby failed to be awed by him as, in later life, he was not awed in the presence of a Field Marshal or Queen Mary and Elizabeth Bowes-Lyon, the only two women he really felt at ease with. An associate of his at St. Paul's was G. K. Chesterton and there is a strong possibility that Tubby was the inspiration for his fictional crime-solving priest "Father Brown" novels. Leonard Browne, who first met him in 1916, spoke of him as:

A pair of spectacles with large black-rimmed glasses; a short, substantial figure; a rather innocent expression on the kindly face — all these combined to make a living embodiment of Mr. Chesterton's famous Father Brown.

At Exeter College, Oxford, Tubby was extremely popular with an insatiable appetite for studying and storing knowledge, which he absorbed like a sponge. Extremely widely read, the printed word was an important part of his world. All of his writings are liberally seasoned with quotes and references, from Cicero to Cervantes, Socrates to Shakespeare, Anthropology to Theology, the Bible to Bunyan. He was also interested in Archaeology, was conversant in both Latin and Ancient Greek and a renowned conversationalist and speaker on well known and obscure topics. At Oxford he habitually used a barber's shop in a little frequented part of the town, and not just for the keen edge of the barber's razor. He enjoyed the sharpness of the barber's mental capabilities and debating skills on a wide variety of subjects. This very nearly cost him his life when, shortly before his final theology examination, he was nicked by a dirty razor and contracted severe blood poisoning. When the time for the examination came he was very ill, his face covered in boils and swellings, and it was only with the help of drugs and the support of friends that he struggled through. When the results were published he was more than a little surprised to find he had been awarded a First Class Degree.

In 1909 Philip left Oxford to study at the Deanery of Westminster as a Young Gentleman of Dean's Yard. Whilst here he wrote a thesis on the mediaeval tiles in the Abbey Sanctuary which, when read to the Society of Antiquities at Burlington, caused him to be made a Fellow of the Society at the comparatively young age of 25. It was at Westminster that he first made contact with the Royal Household. Summoned to the Dean's parlour one afternoon, he took tea with the Princess of Wales and her sons Prince Edward, later King Edward VIII, Duke of Windsor, and Albert, later King George VI. After tea Philip and Trevor Heaton, a fellow Young Gentleman took the young Princes on a tour of the Abbey.

Between 1909 and 1910 he became acquainted with the Docklands area of Bermondsey, devoting much of his spare time and energies to working with the boys' clubs there. 1910, his work in these clubs standing him in good stead, found him Curate of St. Mary's Church, Portsea, working in the slum areas of the parish, a task for which he had a natural aptitude, being able to converse on almost any subject without seeming aloof or patronising. He initiated Bible classes that became bigger than the clubs themselves and, through the teaching of the Bible, helped educate the local men and boys. He introduced confirmation classes whereby after twelve months the communicants took office in the clubs, becoming teachers themselves. He began a summer camp which became an annual success, interrupted only by the outbreak of the Great War.

For a short while in 1914 he became Curate of St. Faith's, a slum area of Portsmouth where he noted:

> . . . this is a rough crowd, . . . but from that tough crowd they won more awards for bravery than the whole parish put together.

He never had the opportunity to develop their potential as, in early 1915, aged 29, he went to France as an Army Chaplain 4th Class.

Spending his first few months on the staff of No. 16 General Hospital at Le Treport, he found his work very depressing, conducting funerals and ministering to the wounded, mostly gas cases for whom very little could be done. Tubby spoke of his first patient, a man named Arthur Green who, after throwing himself onto a grenade to save his officer:

> . . . died slowly limb by limb, a quiet and contented soul.

At the end of the summer he returned to England for a short leave and was replaced by John MacMillan, later Bishop of Dover. On 10th November 1915, embarking from Folkestone he wrote to his mother:

I found myself with three jolly companions, an RAMC doctor, a staff captain from General Headquarters who is going to put me up, or get me to the Deputy Chaplain General tonight, and an HAC chap, who after nine months as a Tommy now comes back as a 2nd Lieut . . . I've never seen the main strength of the British Expeditionary Force before and a most inspiring sight it is. One or two of the men are a bit tipsy, but all the rest are sober and a bit in the dumps, like boys going back to school. One wonders how many of them will see Folkestone again.

Reporting to the Deputy Chaplain General Bishop Gwynne at General Headquarters, Montreuil, Tubby was posted to the 6th Division and found himself in the Ypres Salient with The Buffs (East Kent Regiment) and Bedfordshire Regiment of 16th Infantry Brigade, under Neville Talbot, senior Chaplain to the 6th Division. Neville, a friend from his Oxford days, whose father, Stuart Talbot, Bishop of Winchester, had ordained him in 1911, had been Chaplain of Balliol College for four years and was no stranger to military life, having served with the Cavalry during the Boer War. In 1916 he was promoted to XIV Corps and later to Assistant Chaplain General of the 5th Army.

Tubby wrote at length about the padres of the 6th Division:

In December 1915 the Old Sixth Division, which had trekked up from Armentières in the end of May and had gone out to a so called rest in November, came sadly to the conclusion that they were in for a winter round Ypres. The Division, however, had a tradition that compelled them to make the best of a bad business, and faced the inevitable with that cheerful grousing over minor points which in their philosophy obscured the main misery of the outlook.

While speaking in this black edged tone, I had better introduce you to the Church of England chaplains of the Division at the time. Neville Talbot, the senior chaplain, C. of E., who had taken over some months before, was then busy breaking up the concentration camp of chaplains which had been bequeathed to him, and in marrying off the eligibles into various battalions of their brigade. The exception was H. R. Bates, who was retained at the old chaplains' headquarters (where our horses lived in the farm and we in the stable, to deceive the Boche) to continue his amazing pioneer work within the Church Army Huts. Several of these he built near the camps, largely with his own hands; while forms and tables, stoves and fuel, canteen stores and games he juggled to such purpose that it seemed as if two huts a mile apart shared without knowing it a tea urn and a table on the same day and on the same side of it (The beloved Chaplain Doudney of 16th Infantry Brigade, had been killed at Ypres, October 16th, 1915. Rupert Inglis who succeeded me in the same brigade was killed on the Somme in September 1916).

Meanwhile, padre Reid was adopted by the Queen's Westminsters, Hamer by the Durhams, Wheeler by the York and Lancs, and Kinloch-Jones by the 71st IB, while P. B. Clayton was foisted onto the Buffs and Bedfords, the latter then being out of the line and at rest in Poperinghe.

At this early stage of the BEF, the attachment of chaplains to battalions was still a novelty. At first, all chaplains were attached to medical units only; and those who reached the fighting line were truants from Field Ambulances. Even when there, their task was at the outset confounded with that of an undertaker, and the minister of life was chiefly called upon for burials. Meanwhile, in hospitals, his sole obligation beyond this function was the visiting of those on the daily DI List. Gradually the outlook widened, an amelioration due in no small measure to the example and idealism of Bishop Gwynne, DCG, and the Brigade Chaplain made good. He became at least connected in men's minds with more cheerful rites and a trench going padre made a church going battalion.

7

In November, billeted with the 1st Leicestershire Regiment, he experienced his first sights of war and, concerned with the prospect of having to conduct only parades and funerals, he wrote:

What my own work is to be is not yet decided. Possibly (everything is in a state of flux), I shall be moved back a few miles to run a kind of church hut in a town through which many troops are passing, or I may share the Chaplaincy of the Brigade with a nice Cambridge man here. I am equally happy either way, at present I have very little to do, except try to learn the ropes and the geography, which is complex and vital.

Most of his time he spent visiting the men in the field, braving the shell-damaged roads on a bicycle. On 19th November, on one such sortie, he conducted three services, had tea with a Belgian family, ate a meal with the Army Service Corps and managed to visit a cinema:

. . . and all this with the Germans thundering away on three sides of us.

The division's chaplains held regular meetings where they would discuss ways of better serving the men of the division as a whole. It was at one of these that the idea of a "soldiers' house" was first suggested and steps were taken to bring it into being.

During the week commencing 20th November, Neville Talbot, who had already opened a successful officers' club opposite the railway station in Poperinghe, devoted much of his time and energies towards finding a suitable house. Tubby mentioned this in a letter home:

Friday afternoon, November 27th. Talbot is trying to get an empty house for me in the nearest town (Poperinghe), where I can both live myself and start some kind of homely club for a few of the multitudes of troops who pass to and fro. I'm strongly in favour of this, as it's work that I should be less of a duffer at than this bush brotherhood business with its distracting differences. If it pans out, I shall want a lot of things like papers and pens and pictures (of the "Pears Annual" type) I shall also have a room for a chapel which we badly need for Confirmation work as well as Celebrations.

Whilst he enjoyed his work, with its visits to outlying units, "a trench going padre meant a church going battalion", he felt he could better minister to men, who could not attend in the field, in a more permanent establishment, enabling him to provide services of a more formal nature, allowing men to worship whilst out of the line.

Thus the "Soldier's House" took it's first step to reality.

# CHAPTER
# TWO

# Poperinghe

Will ye go to Flanders, my Mally - o
To see the chief commanders, my Mally - o
You'll see the bullets fly
And the ladies loudly cry,
And the soldiers how they die, my Mally - o.
*18th Century folk song*

The Belgian town of Poperinghe is situated in an agricultural farming area a short distance from the northern border of France and within fifty miles of the Channel ports of Calais and Dunkirk. On 10th August 1914, the German Army marched across Belgium on its way to instigate the invasion of France. Taking advantage of the absence of Allied troops, German High Command had ordered that the area around Ypres should be scouted by cavalry units and, on 4th October, its 3rd Cavalry Brigade (Uhlans), acting as a reconnaissance unit for the 36th Division, entered Poperinghe. On 15th October, the 87th and 89th French Territorial Divisions commanded by General Bidon entered the town causing the Uhlans to move out across the French border to rejoin their division. General Bidon set up his Staff Headquarters and sent his 87th Division directly to Ypres and deployed the 89th in a defensive line between Vlamertinghe and Reninghelst. By the end of November, Poperinghe had become a French garrison town.

In December 1914 British troops had become a common sight in the town as they passed through on their way eastwards to the Ypres Salient. On 1st February 1915 the French Army moved out when the British 6th Division, V Corps, under General Sir Hubert Plumer, took "possession" of the town. From this date onwards Poperinghe was, with the exception of Veurne 20 miles to the northwest, to remain the only free Belgian town behind the front line. On 4th February, it was officially declared part of the British sector and, being the last stop on the Hazebrouck-to-Ypres railway line, the vast majority of troops and equipment on its way to the front passed through it. There was hardly a regiment that did not know "Pop", as the troops soon nicknamed it. Now designated a garrison town, it became a funnel through which division after division passed on their way to the front, and also a town where troops could spend what spare time they had to relax. Vast billeting camps of tents and huts were established in the surrounding area, with munitions dumps and supply depots set up for every calibre of shell and type of equipment required by a modern army. Field kitchens continuously turned out thousands of meals for the ever-hungry soldiers encamped nearby and for those arriving daily. Workshops were established for repairs to the guns and vehicles, and medical facilities and hospitals were established just outside the town, alongside the railway line at Remy Sidings, Abeele and Godewaersvelde.

A number of local châteaux were utilised as military and civilian hospitals, Tubby, visiting one on 22nd March 1916:

I had a very touching experience on Wednesday, of the kind that really helps one. The day before, while I was helping to try and reduce our wilderness into something like the garden it once was, an Abbé accompanied by a Belgian Officer came to call. The purpose of their visit was to ask me to officiate at the funeral of a Belgian Artilleryman who had been killed the night before, and who was believed to be an English Churchman.

The railway station, just within range of the German long range guns, was a favourite target and the town, with its large concentration of British troops, experienced regular night bombing raids. With the exception of one very long range gun nicknamed "Percy", mounted on railway tracks in the vicinity of the Pilckem Ridge north of Ypres, the town was fairly safe from shellfire until the shortening of the Salient in 1915, and the Battle of the Lys in 1918, but aerial activity caused casualties among civilians and military alike. It may not have been the safest place, but to the troops and officers it was a refuge from the relentless misery of trench warfare and the boredom of the camps.

Of his first encounter with Poperinghe Tubby wrote:

I had arrived there one rainy autumn night, fresh from a hospital chaplaincy at Le Treport. The dismal train had crawled cautiously into the station at 2a.m. depositing me with a plethora of luggage at the RTO's office. Leaving my baggage in a hideous heap, and disdaining offers of assistance, I had started to walk, as I thought into Poperinghe with a hazy notion of finding some hotel. Outside the sky was inky overhead and the road deep in mire. Following the crowd of foot passengers back from leave, I had turned in the wrong direction and stepped out along the famous pavé causeway that leads to Vlamertinghe and Ypres. After half an hour's splashing I began to think the town a myth, and upon confiding my thoughts to two men in front was much humbled to discover — 1. I was walking away from Poperinghe, 2. There were no hotels anywhere, 3. I had better go back and ask RTO to take great care of me till called for. This I sadly did, and the RTO, a most kindly man telephoned to such good purpose that before daybreak some London Field Company folk arrived with a mess-cart and removed me to the Chaplain's Camp.

My chief memory of the RTO's office during the waiting was the odd sight of a boy with a Military Medal marched in as a prisoner under escort for return to England, having so falsified his age that he enlisted at sixteen, and had been fighting for six months.

Some months after this initial visit he returned to the town, making completely different observations:

When I returned to Poperinghe, and joined the Bedford's, the town was in typically 1915 condition. There was a canteen in the Square, run by a Wesleyan chaplain, but beyond this nothing but refugee shops, bright behind their rabbit-wire windows. Of course, there were estaminets everywhere, good, bad and of all intermediate complexions. The town at the time was intermittently shelled but "nothing to write home about". Some very heavy "Stuff" had come in during the early summer when the fashionable area of the town was in consequence constantly changing. One large shell had completely demolished the original English Church house, near the Square. The wealthier "civil" population had moved into France, and the remainder, chiefly refugees, were busily engaged in amassing wealth under circumstances adverse to the prosperity of their insurance companies. One combined pastry cook and brewery concern was said to have made £5,000 clear profit in four months.

In 1919, under the pseudonym "Rev. Verdant Green, CF", he wrote of the town:

Poperinghe, so the only guidebook that troubles itself with the little town tells us, contains some 11,000 inhabitants, and no features of interest for the visitor. The war modified the accuracy of both these statements. The population of the town and its immediate environs has risen at times to a quarter of a million, and has fallen to less than fifty. As for features of interest, the orderly room clerks could give the evidence of tens of thousands of passes to the contrary. The name of the town might as well have been printed in, for all the correction it was likely to require.

The secret of this was that Poperinghe was without a rival locally. Alone free for years among Belgian towns, close enough to the line to be directly accessible to the principal sufferers, and not so near as to be positively ruinous, it became metropolitan not by merit but by the logic of locality. In migrant and mobile times, its narrow and uneven streets filled and foamed with a tide race of transport. Year in, year out, by night and by day, the fighting troops, with all the blunter forces behind that impel and sustain their operations, set east and west, with that rhythm of fluctuation that stationary war induces. Until the great switch road was opened and every mule (whether on four legs or closely packed in a blue "bully beef" tin) came up by one pair of rails or one narrow street. Moreover, before the camps were built, troops billeted in the town itself in huge number, prudently decreased as the thing called bombing grew in ease and frequency of performance.

It was an odd, but not an evil atmosphere which prevailed in Pop. Every week some shells landed somewhere, and some lives were lost; but the spirit of lightheartedness was never quenched, nor was there on the other side, any outbreak of vice behind the gaiety. In spite of the gigantic accumulation of troops, rape was almost unknown, and seduction extremely rare — to the amazement, I believe, of the Belgian authorities. War, was still a sporting event, and "living dangerously" was salutary, as Nietzsche taught. The ethics of home were not blurred by long absence, and the Russian "steam roller" was not yet ditched. No prospect pleased, but man was perfectly glorious.

# CHAPTER
# THREE

# Flanders Inn

It had about it the homely flavour of a village inn, and for its deeper note there was the thought of the commemoration of Gilbert Talbot . . .

*Philip Clayton*

From the very outset of the British Army's involvement with Poperinghe, and its subsequent development into a garrison town, it had been the intention of the military authorities to provide the men with an alternative place of relaxation to the many cafés and estaminets. There were already a Y.M.C.A. establishment and a number of Church Army huts situated in and around the town. In late November 1915, Neville Talbot, in his searching for suitable premises, had the family house of a certain Mr Coevoet-Camerlynck, a local businessman, brought to his attention. The owner had decided to remove himself and his family from Poperinghe for the duration of the war. A deciding factor in his departure may well have been a direct hit by a 5.9 inch shell, damaging the roof and one room of the house. Whatever the reason, in the subsequent negotiations, the damage repair was made part of the tenancy agreement, as was the odd request for the removal of a large safe from a small downstairs room at the front of the house.

Tubby wrote:

It was plain that it was up to the chaplains to open a place of their own, an institutional church, to provide happiness for the men and also if possible, a hostel for officers going on leave. This trouble, like all our troubles, was taken to Col. R. S. May, Quartermaster of the 6th Division. Aided wholeheartedly by him, we approached the Town Major, who introduced us to Mr Coevoet-Camerlynck, a wealthy brewer of the town, who in turn led us to his great empty mansion, the back part of which had recently been struck by a shrapnel shell from the Pilckem Ridge direction. We accepted this tenancy joyfully, at a rent which was subsequently fixed at 150 francs a month, undertaking as the conditions of our lease — 1. to make the house weatherproof, 2. to remove from the small front room a large safe, which on account of its immobility, had remained when all the other furniture had been taken away.

Strong in the consciousness of the British Army at our backs, we made no bones about the conditions, but took over the House forthwith. Bowing the owner out, we started on our inspection of the premises. The large entrance hall was flanked on the left by a highly decorative drawing-room with a dingy dining-room beyond, and on the right by a small office, the staircase, and the kitchen. The conservatory beyond lay sideways along the whole breadth of the House at the back. It was in a bad plight, for the shrapnel had gashed its leaden roof and brought down the plaster ceiling in a melancholy ruin upon its tiled floor. The plate glass was broken in all the windows, and the rain came in freely both sideways and from above. However, it's an ill shell that blows no one any good, and this had blown us a house which would otherwise have been occupied as a billet. Upstairs on the first floor, reached by an elegant painted staircase in white and gold, was the landing, four bedrooms, and a dressing room; on the second floor, a large landing, one huge nursery, and three small bedrooms; above this, reached by a difficult companion-ladder, a great hop-loft covering the whole area of the house. One corner of this attic, and the bedroom below it, had been knocked out by a shell.

He also noted:

Tuesday November 30th 1915 . . . I am very busy living with one of my battalions in billets and taking over a jolly house which is to be the Pusey House of the place when we have swept it out and bunged the hole where the shell hit it.

On 1st December, full of enthusiasm about the house, he referred to himself as "a kind of innkeeper". This was noticed by Captain Leonard Browne who, in August 1916, wrote:

But what of Boniface himself? The good Prince of Innkeepers would recognise mine host of Talbot House as not least among his children. A history of the House would be incomplete without some delineation of the characteristics of the publican himself, so a physician has taken up the task, despite the objections of Boniface.

Clayton was delighted with this and wrote:

Thus with a flow of antiquated courtesies, the landlord welcomed his distinguished guests; and regretting that nature had long ago deprived him of that waist without which a posture of deference cannot be well attempted, ushered their excellencies into Talbot House.

On the 2nd December, General, The Earl of Cavan, Commanding XIV Corps, on a tour of inspection, made a visit to the house. Tubby only heard of the visit the night before and, apart from a reading room and a small chapel, he had very little to show the General. As it was, he was more preoccupied with weeding the garden than entertaining a visiting General. About this time he was also occupied in honouring the tenancy agreement:

The safe was in the little front office, and presented the appearance of a large brown painted cupboard against the wall. Neville gave it a friendly push, with no result whatever. My assistance made not the slightest difference. I stepped round the corner for the Bedfords. About sixteen of them came in an SOS spirit. As many as could do so got near the safe and pushed perspiringly. The faintest sign of motion was now visible. Determined to see the matter through at once, lest it should breed in us some craven superstition, we suborned certain transport folk to send round their heaviest wagon and a team of mules. Meanwhile we got ropes round the safe and some logs, as for launching a lifeboat. With sixteen men on the rope the safe fell forward onto the rollers with a crash comparable only with the coup de grace the Australian tunnellers gave to Hill 60. Crowds gathered in the narrow street, and the wagon and mules made heavy weather of backing into the entrance of the House. Meanwhile we piloted the safe into the hall. The mules were taken out and led away that they might not see what they were doomed to draw. The back of the wagon was let down, the stoutest planks were laid leading up to it, and the drag ropes were handed freely to all passers by. Vaguely it was felt by all who had no precise knowledge of the situation that a successful tug would in some way shorten the war; and the traffic, now completely blocked, added to those homely criticisms for which the British driver is justly notable. Even the safe felt moved in its rocky heart, and surrendering to the impulse of a hundred hands, found itself installed in the wagon. It was no time for hesitancy now. Pressing ten francs into the hands of the muleteers, we told them the desired destination and saw them and the safe no more.

Another task that came within the tenancy agreement was the making good of the shell damage. This was attended to within the first few days, when a party of Royal Engineers boarded over the exterior damage whilst men of the Queen's Westminster Rifles repaired the shell splintered floor, patching it with flattened and nailed down biscuit tins.

Tubby found a much used carpenter's bench in the garden out-house. He regularly referred to Jesus Christ as the Carpenter's Son and felt that no more fitting object could better serve as an altar than this bench. After being given a much needed cleaning it was installed in the chapel where it served as the altar throughout the remainder of the war.

Colonel R. S. May, Assistant Adjutant, Quarter Master General, 6th Division visited the house while Tubby was in the process of having a sign made for the building. The wording was not very imaginative and the popular story, as related by Tubby in a letter of 5th December 1915, has it that the Colonel said:

Church House? Won't do at all — enough to choke anyone off. Why not Talbot House christened, if not after the unwilling Neville, to perpetuate the memory and spirit of a subaltern dead five months before? Talbot House — Forthwith in the mouths of men it is and will remain.

Later Tubby wrote:

We had, after many wild suggestions, agreed on some tame and noncommittal title, and having contrived six feet of stretched canvas, were busy on the first letter of "Church House", when Colonel May arrived and announced that the House should be closed there and then if we did not call it Talbot House. Despite Neville's protests, the name was fixed forthwith. This version of the story later states that the House was named after Gilbert Talbot at Colonel May's insistence.

A letter written by the Colonel in 1943 concerning the name suggests something different. It reads:

May I correct an error in your article on Neville Talbot in the May JOURNAL? My memory on the subject is quite clear. The 6th Division went to the Ypres Salient in April, 1915, and were billeted in the Poperinghe area. Neville was Senior Chaplain and I was AA, C in C of the Division. The padres lived in A15 outside Poperinghe. During my daily tour of the divisional area I discovered that both the Roman Catholic and Methodist padres had comfortable quarters in which they provided food, periodicals and writing materials for the troops, whereas the C of E padres had done nothing. I went to Neville in May and told him I thought the C of E ought to establish something for the troops on the lines of the other denominations and I would willingly provide the accommodation. He agreed and said he would think it over. As his plans did not mature I asked him, repeatedly, if he was taking action. He replied "Yes," but at the moment could not get the man he wanted to run the house. Thus it was not until December that the house was opened. I happened to be passing along the Rue de l'Hopital at the time two or three men were erecting the sign "Church House". I stopped my car, went in, and told Neville that such a sign would frighten away the very men he wanted to attract. I did not mind what the house was called so long as it was not called "Church House", and suggested that he should call it after his own name. He did so, but really dedicated it to his brother, of whose death I was ignorant. Some years afterwards his father, Bishop Talbot, asked me how the house got the name of Talbot House and I told him the above story.

Thus Talbot House, named after Neville Talbot was dedicated by him to his youngest brother Lieutenant Gilbert W. L. Talbot, 7th Battalion, The Rifle Brigade, killed at Hooge, 30th July 1915.

Before the house opened an amount of furniture was installed, a table made from two tent floor-boards found in the garden and covered with wall paper, together with a number of chairs, built from packing cases. Cups, saucers and other items were purchased from:

... a half ruined shop opposite, where a Belgian boy named Gerard and his mother and sister carried on their business, though the staircase and most of the first floor had succumbed to a shell. Climbing one day on to what was left of the second floor, I found and purchased for three francs a crucifix, the figure (as so often locally) of white clay, with a hand splintered by a fragment of the shell.

Taking time off from his work with the Church Army huts Harold Bates, another 6th Division chaplain, became a regular member of the staff. His early association with the house was sadly cut short when on 19th December:

Dear Bates, one of the six padres of the Division, got his leg broken about five minutes after leaving us ... rescuing a small child from an aeroplane bomb; he's quite alright but it's a two months job, so we are very shorthanded for Christmas.

From Talbot House. Monday, 6th December, Tubby wrote:

Talbot has given me the job of opening a kind of Church House here in a town full of troops, some permanent like police, Signal Co's, R.E.'s, R.A.M.C., ASC, etc., others coming in and going out on their way up. True the Boche are less than ten miles away on three sides of us, and don't let us forget it from time to time. But if they shell this place, one or other of their own billets gets a return of the compliment with interest from our "heavies". So that the game is, on the whole, unprofitable from their point of view . . .

It is a beautiful house with a lovely garden, full of standard roses, pergolas, wall-fruit and a chicken run. I'm going to get together a little batch of amateur gardeners to run the garden in spare time — it will be a peaceful relaxation, much appreciated and I'm anxious to have the place in apple-pie order. After the voluntary service last night (held in a music hall) about forty men came round with me and went over the house, which was great fun and made them quite keen on it all. We have an inaugural Concert on Saturday night . . . Meanwhile as I write, a stream of traffic, like that of Fleet Street passes slowly — staff cars, motor cyclists, lorries, wagons, horsemen, ambulances, soldiers of all sorts and descriptions, carts with furniture of refugees who can stand it no longer (probably when the real risk is over) tied on precariously. I covet these chairs and tables greatly. Meanwhile papers and books from time to time will be a real help. The men here are grateful for the simplest kindness shown to them personally: a cup of cocoa and a Belgian bun do not lack their reward.

And on 15th December:

A good deal has happened since last week. You will notice in the first place that the name of the house has changed for the better — this was a command from Divisional HQ, and has been carried out in spite of Talbot's protests. I am glad, as a Junior Chaplain, to find that there are men so resolute in high command that they can impose their will on the Senior Chaplain! Moreover, he deserves it, and his name is one to conjure with on all sides. Secondly the house is now open in two departments out of three. The men's part accommodating about a hundred for reading, writing and arithmetic, opened on Saturday, with a sing-song at which I sang the ditty about "sixteen blades and a corkscrew" . . . Another sphere of the house's work accounts for my being up tonight. I have just sent my first two weary travellers to bed, after soup and biscuits, and they will have excellent breakfasts in the morning before they go on their way rejoicing this is the opening of our divisional rest-house, to which officers coming and going by trains in the small hours can come and get supper, bed and breakfast. Tonight, being the first time, I went up to the station with the very nice night orderly — I now control a staff of three men under an NCO besides my own, Pettifer — and rescued these two from a cold night in the waiting-room (so called). We can accommodate twelve and shall have the house full every night a week hence, when it is known. Both were profoundly grateful, and were nearly moved to tears by the carpet slippers awaiting them. The third department of the house — the "Officers' Clubroom" — is not ready yet, but will be, I hope, in a few days — and all this within a few miles of the German lines.

Very quickly the house became known as Toc H, a name taken from signaller's code of the time. Toc' for the "T" of Talbot and "H" for the "H" in House. The original *Talbot House 1915–? Every Man's Club.* sign still hangs above the front doors of the house; welcoming today's visitor in exactly the same way as it did during the war years. From its conception the house was always intended to be a place to relax. Non-denominational and offering ministry to every man no matter what his rank or leaning. Life in the Ypres Salient was a great leveller, a shell splinter or a bullet showed no discrimination and death was the greatest leveller of them all. The military cemeteries all bear silent testimony to this, a Major lays next to a Corporal, a Captain alongside a Sergeant, a Colonel by Private and so on. Every man had as much chance of survival as his fellow. Prior to the Great War, Britain was a "social class" structured nation with the divisions separating the classes strictly adhered to. The classes kept themselves, for the most part, totally detached from each other. The war changed this. It is true that most of the officers came from the upper classes but equally true that a high percentage of them served in the ranks, refusing commissions offered purely because of their social standing. The evidence of these men alone speaks for itself, they all shared the same dangers. If Life and Death showed no discrimination, why should a house?

The *1915–?* was a way of stating the date of establishment with the date of "closure" being uncertain. The house would be available to the British for the duration of the war or until such time as its owner returned. Whatever the case, the *1915–?* left the question unanswered,

On 11th December 1915, the eve of Tubby's 30th birthday, Talbot House officially opened and, apart from a short spell in 1918, remained so for the next three years. During that time Everyman's Club welcomed all comers with few exceptions. Having entered, the visitor was greeted by the same sign that greets the visitor today, a hand pointing back into the street with the words *To Pessimists Way Out* printed around it.

A small staff was allocated to the house, initially an NCO and three men from the 17th Field Ambulance which, with Tubby and his barman totalled six. After four months the Field Ambulance staff returned to their unit and thereafter the staff, with the exception of Tubby and Pettifer, were of a semi permanent nature:

... and replaced by Guardsmen under Sergeant Godley of the Coldstreamers. Some humourist on GHQ had arranged at the time — April 1916 — that the Guards and the Canadians should occupy the town together, and the result was as instructive as it was amusing. In the Guards area, to a civilian encountering them for the first time, the feeling was one of dismay. NCO's and privates were unable to share the same rooms, and when one resumed from shopping in their quarter of the town, the problem of returning salutes while leading home a primus stove, however lawfully purchased, was harassing to the last degree. Ultimately I became so nervous of these ordeals that I walked only by night in the Guards area, and then said "Friend" hurriedly in the dark to the buttresses of the church. In the Canadian area there was no such shyness, though in their later days saluting became, I believe, quite in vogue with them also. Yet the Guards were not only admirable; they were lovable. In no division that came our way was there so strong a family feeling. There was rivalry, but it was a rivalry towards a common ideal. There was hard and minute discipline, but the task was hard before them. The officers would do anything for their men, and the adjutant knew them and their home circumstances sometimes to the third generation. Even the R.S.M. would unbend enough to ask of a man resuming from leave when Jim would be ripe for Caterham, and how the old man was doing. Of surviving Guardees who were true Talbothousians I cannot speak freely, but one of our best friends was Lieutenant Guy Dawkins, of 2nd Scots Guards, who had taken his commission thither from the London Scottish. A critic of men better qualified would have been hard to find, for his reputation stood high before the war in the LAC, and he was so deeply possessed by the fighting spirit that he died more of disappointment than of his wound early in the Somme offensive. It was he who discovered to me the fact so hard for the civilian mind to grasp — that in the very fixity of the gulf between each grade of command lay the scope for an intimacy and mutual understanding impossible otherwise. Elsewhere the younger officer might feel that too much solicitude for his men might prejudice his caste; but here, where he was almost of another clay, he could and indeed must, take their comfort and welfare as his supreme concern.

Of the many conquests of the Guards in this war, none was more complete than that of Talbot House. We dreaded their arrival, but longed for their return. The House was never more so musical as when Quarter-Master Sergeant Randall brought in his glee party of Welsh Guards, so numerous that there was scarcely room for the audience; nor in domestic matters, were the floors ever so spotless, the lamps so well trimmed, or the garden so neat, as under the regime of Sergeant Godley.

A few weeks before the Somme began, it became clear that the House could no longer stand the strain of its double obligation both to officers and men; so we bombed the officers out, and, with the modesty of padres, took over for the exiles the premises of "A" Mess of the Guards Division in a house hard by. Here and thus the Officers' Club

31

Poperinghe, began under the control of Neville Talbot. Subsequently, to meet the manifold problems of catering, etc., in view of the tremendous concentration in 1917, it was handed over to the EFC, who maintained it until the evacuation in the Spring of the following year.

Scarcely was this new house opened than the Somme swept Guards and Canadians alike southwards, and the salient became for the first time in its history a quiet spot for weakened divisions to maintain. Hitherto the average number of daily casualties passing through the Casualty Clearing Stations in the district had been seldom less than 200. From that time to the following February even Ypres was a place well suited to open air exercise.

The Somme brought us an unexpected blessing in the persons of two old Q.W.R. friends, who after their contribution to the regiment's costly participation down south, came up to recuperate in what was then known as an entrenching battalion. By the courtesy of the CO, the House was able to attach them to its staff until they were both fit to rejoin the regiment — they were both then commissioned. Needless to say, their presence cemented the old associations and reintroduced the old atmosphere. The library grew more prodigiously, so that the catalogue was always inferior to the reality. Debates, whist-drives, classes, and the standard of musical taste, leapt up as if by magic. This was our happiest winter, for the divisions in occupation at the time included 38th, 39th, 47th and 55th, and among them many enduring and undeviating friendships were discovered.

With the coming of the Spring, 1917, the preparations for the Messines offensive brought the House new friends as well as old. The 23rd Division, which subsequently went to Italy, counted its Talbothousians by hundreds; and in the ominous interval prolonged past all endurance, while the Fifth Army and the French came up for July 31st, and everyone said "Hush" at the tops of their voices, the House reached the zenith of its activity. In a single day 500 francs were taken in 1d. cups of tea alone. Meanwhile the 8th Corps had built us a concert-hall, ingeniously contrived out of an adjoining hop-store. The lawns of the delightful garden were brown with men basking like lizards in the sun; the staff of the House was augmented to seventeen — its maximum strength. The 18th Corps appointed a committee of management, which did yeoman service, under Major Bowes of the Cambridgeshires; and the 19th Corps headed our subscription list with 1,000 francs. The House was repapered at least twice a week, and repainted on alternate Tuesdays. A test tally of ten minutes duration at the front door revealed the entry of 117 men; and thus we lived through the summer during which so many of our best friends died, and came with set teeth to that unforgettable autumn when division after division went forward almost to drown, that those eternal slopes might at last be won, which had the weather held, might have been ours in the first week of August.

In the late twenties Tubby was to write:

There was less said about the war in Talbot House than probably anywhere else in Europe at the time. As a topic it had its limitations, like the weather. As a conversational opening its vagaries were of value, but no more than that, the real thing was to get relief from it, relief comic, serio-comic, educational, spiritual.

He rarely mentioned or expressed opinion about the war itself; yet his narratives are full of references to certain actions, units and individuals. To the men of both the British Expeditionary Force and later to "Kitchener's Battalions", Talbot House was not only special for a variety of reasons but was also unique. Tubby realised this from the very early days of its existence:

Even within the Army at the close, the Old House became rather a back number in the back area, and the Armistice generation had Meccas of its own. Yet their elder brothers cheered the sign board as they marched down the street, and Second Lieutenant T. Smithkinson-Browne in 1917 would hark back half shyly to the haunts of Rifleman Tom

Brown of 1916, with the loyalty of an old schoolboy revisiting those grey towers that nursed him in his teens. Divisions trekking northwards from the Somme were known to count proximity to Talbot House as some measure of compensation for a return to the Salient, for the boredom of the Somme wilderness was a more fearful thing than fear itself.

Lieutenant-Colonel F. R. Barry who visited in 1917 recorded:

... in the white house next to the Officers' Club was the most remarkable thing in the BEF ... I can only say what "Everyman's Club" felt like to one among many thousand other pilgrims who found reason for undying gratitude to the House, and all it did for him. For its record is a radiant history of light and fellowship and joy and laughter breaking into the darkness of the Salient. For countless men, to pass inside that door has been to enter into a new world — the world of all the things that are really true — and to know that all without was a long nightmare. Toil as we might, the various recreation rooms which we tried to organise for troops were still conspicuously lacking in something not too easy to define. They were far too much like Institutions, their horrible six-foot tables and long forms shouting at you, shrink from it as you would, that they had kindly been arranged by someone to amuse (or pacify) our heroes. They were perfectly good Institutes. This was different: it was a home. That was the distinctive thing about it. All round the cinemas and concerts said to men, "Come inside and forget". Talbot House had the audacity to invite us all to enter — and remember. It recalled to us forgotten things. It brought us face to face with ourselves again, revived in us again the men we were before our personalities were merged in the impersonal drive of the machine. We too were men, with immortal longings in us. We too had each of us our history, our hopes and fears and pains and aspirations; and here we could renew ourselves again. So it was that the House lives in the memory of a tale of men that will never be fully told, as the place where they recovered faith and hope, and first began to dare to believe in love.

Imagine what it meant to the British soldier! To be able to lie back in a real armchair, and sleep, or read, or talk as he felt inclined, not to be "pushed about" by anybody, to know he was expected to do as he would. To have the run of a really first rate library and take up old-time intellectual interests. To be surrounded by a refined comfort which took him and his goodwill for granted, forcing nothing and obtruding nothing, but treating him with that confident respect that is the one indestructible "right of man". Such things impressed even the unimpressionable, and the first taste of them was not soon forgotten. These things were to be found in the antechambers; but the genius of the House was something bigger, and it was found by all who were seeking for it. It was the gift of spiritual fellowship. The frequenters of the Club were more than Clubmen. They were an ever-widening Brotherhood.

On a visit to Poperinghe, Douglas Legg "discovered" Talbot House:

Through an elaborate, iron grilled, doorway I could hear the sound of laughter and music. On pushing through the door I found myself at once in a different world. It was amazing. I felt like Alice when she stepped through the looking-glass. There were soldiers all around me, of course, and army slang in the air, but, in stepping across that threshold, I seemed to have left behind me all the depression and weariness of the street.

Tubby, always enthusiastic to write about the house, adds:

Men swarmed about the place from 10a.m. to 8p.m., and officers flowed in from 7p.m. till the leave trains came and went. From each officer we demanded five francs for board and lodging, on the Robin Hood principle of taking from the rich to give to the poor. For this sum the officers secured on arrival from the leave train at 1a.m. cocoa and Bath Oliver biscuits, or before departure at 5a.m. a cold meat breakfast.

The provision of overnight accommodation for officers going on, or returning from, leave was exploited by Tubby. Difference between the military class structure was radically changed by Talbot House. Between 7 and 8p.m. King's Regulations dictated military protocol be strictly observed. This was neither possible nor practical in the house. Many officers had relatives and friends amongst the ranks, N.C.O.'s had friends amongst the officers and other ranks alike and some troops chose only to salute officers of their own regiment. Tubby, foreseeing problems, set a house rule: *All Rank Abandon Ye Who Enter Here*. It was radical for 1916, but it worked. Initially it applied only within the Chaplain's Room itself, but soon became practice throughout the house.

He had also decided that visitors to the house should have a piano at their disposal. At one time Charles Doudney had what he chose to describe as a "looted" piano and, had he survived, it is probable this would have been installed. However, at the inaugural concert on 10th December Tubby enquired of the audience if anyone knew of the whereabouts of a "spare" piano. A Royal Artillery major told him that he knew a Lieutenant Robinson, 47th Battery, who had at least three of them. The next day Tubby contacted Chaplain Kinloch-Jones, of 71st Infantry Brigade, with instructions to look for a piano. Later he was given a message addressed to Kinloch-Jones requesting that he meet Lieutenant Robinson at 41st Infantry Brigade Headquarters, at 11.30a.m. the following morning. As the 41st's headquarters were outside the 6th Division's area Tubby needed a travel-pass to get there. Neglecting to obtain the necessary paperwork, he decided to use the letter addressed to Kinloch-Jones as a pass instead. Once at the headquarters he made his way to the officers' mess and informed the duty officer he was to meet with Lieutenant Robinson, at which point he was asked for his pass. Seeing the letter, the subaltern mistakenly took him to be Kinloch-Jones. Deciding that discretion be the better part of valour, and not wishing to be "taken for a spy", Tubby accepted his new name. In the meantime, Lieutenant Robinson, on his way to the meeting, was inadvertently taken to Jimmy Reid, padre to the Queen's Westminster Rifles. On realising the mistake, both men then went in search of Tubby and, on finding him, they referred to him as Clayton, only to find themselves corrected by the mess subaltern with a curt "Kinloch-Jones not Clayton". Choosing to avoid the complications of a lengthy explanation, it was thought best not to confuse the young officer. After all was sorted out, Tubby's effort was rewarded with two pianos. The popular version of this story says there were three and that "Tubby sold the other two to help pay the rent". In reality there were only two and, selecting one, Tubby gave the other, "the worst one", to his fellow padre Harold Bates for use in a Church Army hut at Peselhoek:

D. Eardley-Wilmot said of the piano kept for Talbot House:

The best was very good indeed . . . and even in its old age, after three years of constant strumming, retained its tone. Moreover, it had learnt things. If

**39**

you so much as sat down before it in 1918, it played "A Little Grey Home In The West" without further action on your part.

Tubby wasn't averse to using his influence in high places in his quest for equipping the house and, by all accounts, he was also adept in the old soldier's art of "scrounging". If he specifically needed anything, it would generally materialise. He was more than a little pleased with himself and his skills as a "scrounger", testifying to it quite openly:

"Give me the luxuries of life, and I care not who has the necessities" was the motto of the young House. We had a piano, but no dishcloths, to the great scandal of a visiting ADMS. But by degrees we accumulated even these. A lady bountiful in Scotland sent us crates of furniture without number, and provisions without price. It is hard to remember the days when dainty food came pouring out from home. A lady in Bristol showered other good and useful things upon us. A third in Brighton, and a fourth at Teddington, found us in books and pictures. Curtains and tablecloths, pots and pans, even wastepaper baskets and clocks and flower vases arrived in illogical sequence.

Many of his acquisitions were donations and gifts from influential friends and the families of officers, but a like amount would also have been donated by the families of other ranks and from his mother who was very supportive of her son's activities at Talbot House.

Sister Alison MacFie, V.A.D., a frequent visitor, wrote of this:

> Friends at home, led by Mrs Clayton, Tubby's mother, kept the stream of supplies constantly moving and put their prayers as well as their hearts into their work. Others who helped were relatives and friends of men who used Talbot House. They received letters written from there telling of the friendship found, the beauty and peace of the garden, the humour of the notices, the comfort and peace of the Upper Room. They knew what this meant and were grateful and wished to help.

Julian Bickersteth, Senior Chaplain, 56th Division, in his approval of what Talbot House meant to the troops of the 56th said:

> 20th August 1916 ... It is a large house in the centre of the town and fitted up splendidly. There are reading rooms, writing rooms, a library, quiet rooms, card rooms, canteen, café, open-air lounge, garden, concert room, and every possible device for making the soldier comfortable. Delightful pictures cover the walls, and facetious remarks are pinned up at various places by the altogether admirable chaplain-in-charge, imploring those who use the club not to remove all the writing paper from the writing room or otherwise pillage the club.

Similarly, from Lieutenant Burgon Bickersteth, 1st Royal Dragoons:

It is a big rambling kind of house in the main street leading from the square towards Cassel. At its large open doors blackboards give the latest war news. On the left inside is a canteen, and rooms with pianos, and straight through, a garden with tables and chairs and hammocks, where tired men can rest. The whole place is for men — no officers admitted.

and later:

This is wrong. Of course officers were admitted.

# CHAPTER
# FOUR

# Welcome to All
# Who Enter

What shall they know of Talbot House
Who only know the ground floor know
*Rudyard Kipling*

The transformation, from its beginnings in late 1915, with only the barest and most basic of fixtures and fittings, into a "homely" place for officers and men alike to visit was achieved gradually. Most furniture and fittings date from 1916–1917, but items were continually being installed — some as late as 1918. The rooms on the ground floor: the hall; a large sitting room; dining room; conservatory running across the entire length of the rear; kitchen; small front room and the wide entrance hall bisecting from front to rear, all had individual functions during different periods of the war.

**The Hall**, pretty much as it was during the war, today has a framed 1916 map which belonged to the 162nd Heavy Battery, Royal Garrison Artillery hanging on the wall to the left of the front doors. Heavily stained and in some places completely obliterated by constant finger-ing, it was kept safely for the house by Padre Humphrey Money, Chaplain's Force (New Zealand), who, for a short time in 1917, was in charge of the house. Other memorabilia on the walls include a framed copy of the front page of the *Daily Sketch* newspaper dated 5th January, 1915 featuring a story on the 1914 Christmas Truce held at nearby Ploegsteert, and a print of Will Longstaff's *The Menin Gate At Midnight* with, alongside it, the poem of the same title written for the house in his later years by Donald Hodge ex-7th Battalion, Royal West Kent Regiment.

A regular visitor to the house in the years following, both before and after the Second World War, Donald Hodge recalled:

In the autumn of 1917 I noticed a horse drawn limber which bore the logo of my brother's division. He was a driver in the Field Artillery, and his horselines would be the place to find him. By devious means I discovered the lines and made my way to see him. Having met, we made arrange-ments, when duty allowed, to meet on a certain date in Poperinghe, where I heard one could have a cup of tea, as, both being total abstainers, an estaminet was out of the question. So in the dark of night we made our rendezvous, met with joy and enjoyed our cuppa, in what could be no other than Talbot House.

I said to him: "We should send something to Mother. Have you got any money?" "No," he replied, "haven't you?" We found we were both in the same position, but between us we found three francs which was just enough for a silk edged postcard to send home to the best of mothers, with our love. Long after, we learned the joy it gave to Mum and Dad.

On prominent display on one wall in the hall is a notice board constructed from two pieces of wood giving a potted history of the house compiled by Tubby.

To the left of the above is a portrait photograph of Gilbert Talbot in uniform and, to the right, a profile sketch of Tubby in 1919 by Sir William Rothenstein, entitled *The Innkeeper*. Nearby is a memorial panel to Major Paul Slessor.

At the base of the stairs is the notice board that welcomed the early pilgrims to Talbot House.

One of two frequently updated notice boards during the war, this one "The Notice Board" carried information, in the most part, from the fertile pen of Tubby himself. These were designed to be both informative and instructive to the first-time visitor. In many cases they were of a serious nature, written in a humorous manner. Whatever their content they were eagerly read by the men and then discarded. A few survived, and now hang framed in the House.

When Douglas Legg first became acquainted with the house he noted,

... there were soldiers all around me and army slang in the air. There were walls with paper on them, clean paper too, carpeted stairs, pictures on the walls and vases with flowers in them. I paused long enough to scan some, at any rate, of the wise and witty injunctions on the notice board. No "Do Not Spit" notices were here but the human invitation, *If you are in the habit of spitting on the carpets at home, please spit here.*

The second board, called "Friendship Corner" was used to help find, pass messages to, or give information about, friends, relations and colleagues. A notice, originally affixed to this board read:

This Board is intended for the use of men who wish to get into touch with friends, who may possibly see a message left for them. Please use cards provided or put communications in an envelope before placing in the rack.

A number of notes from this board that survived the war were framed and presented to the house on 20th September 1997.

**The Sitting Room** was for a short time during the war Tubby's quarters until, in Spring 1916, he moved to the first floor. It became the Tea Bar where soldiers were served tea or coffee from two huge urns. With this room supplying the men's first need, Tubby's move upstairs served to place him closer to administering their second.

From October 1918 until the Armistice the Sitting Room housed the library.

During the years when the house had a resident warden, this and the adjoining room, served as private quarters. Today it serves as a shop for Talbot House souvenir items and books on the Ypres Salient. In the evenings it serves, once more, as a sitting room for the duty wardens. On the walls are letters and philatelic "First Day Covers" showing the strong ties with the British Royal Family. On 13th May 1966 Her Majesty Queen Elizabeth II, with HRH Prince Philip, Duke of Edinburgh and the Belgian King Boudewijn I visited, and HRH Princess Alexandria of Kent did so on 22nd April 1985. The Belgian King Albert II came on 26th September 1996. Katrien Louagie-Nolf, of the Friends of Talbot House, wrote:

There seems to be no end to the long row of prominent visitors to Talbot House. The 80th Anniversary of the Battle of Passchendaele and the 70th Anniversary of the Inauguration of the Menin Gate did not only bring HRH Prince Philip of Belgium to our part of the country, but also HRH the Duke of Kent. At this occasion the Duke also popped into Pop. Only a visit to the Upper Room had been planned, but the Duke was so interested that he wanted a full tour of the House. After he had signed the Visitor's Book, he had a chat with the guests in the garden. On behalf of the Association, Mrs Duclos presented him with a beautiful picture of the Upper Room . . .

On one wall, a framed photograph of a barely 5-foot tall Tubby standing outside the house with a 6-foot 5-inch Neville Talbot highlights what a strange sight they appeared when together.

Bruce Bairnsfather, the creator of "Old Bill", often visited Poperinghe and, in a display cabinet in the room, there is a fine selection of Staffordshire China plates decorated with his cartoons.

A frequent visitor to the house during the latter part of the war, Eric Kennington donated three of his studies after the Armistice which take pride of place in the house. In the early nineties a number of items disappeared, one of them being his renowned *Grave of Man*. It was later found well hidden behind bookshelves in the local library and returned to its rightful place.

**The Dining Room** has three points of entry. The first, by way of two gilded doors leading from the sitting room, the second through two glazed doors from the conservatory and the third a door from the hallway. For a while this room served as an extension of the Tea Bar and from October 1918 as a billiard room. During the intervening period it served as an Officers' Room, complete with a piano. Today, after alternating for many years between a private sitting room and dining room it is used mostly for the latter or as a meeting room.

**The Kitchen**, its original position being where the ground floor toilets are, was much smaller than today's. It then, as now, operated as a self-catering unit. Fully equipped, it was at the disposal of visiting troops, providing they had the requisite ingredients, under the proviso "Leave the kitchen as you would wish to find it!" It was said to be so well equipped that what it didn't contain "hadn't been invented yet!"

Today it occupies the site of what was originally the "Kitchen Garden Sitting Room" a section of which was used to grow salad vegetables, stored in a greenhouse environment. The remaining section served as a conservatory for a variety of recreational and educational purposes: poetry classes; Shakespeare readings; "Lantern" slide shows and whist drives. It was also known as the ground floor Writing Room.

**The Office** is the room where Tubby, Neville and five men pushed, shoved and tugged-out the Coevoet-Camerlynck safe and for a period in late 1918, it served as the Chapel. A notice, dated 1st October reads:

Old friends of the House will find the old arrangements rudely disturbed for the time being. The old Chapel is temporarily dismantled, and the Chapel, always open as ever, is in the room on the ground floor behind the tubular bells. Evensong daily at 6.30p.m.
P.B.C.

**The Conservatory**, providing a sheltered view to the garden, was severely damaged by a 5.9 inch shell. Its leaded roof was ripped and torn, the ceiling below cracked and its plaster deposited on the floor, with all the windows broken. Within a short time Tubby's band of helpers cleared the debris and made good the roof. To keep the weather out the windows were repaired with oiled linens stretched and tacked to the existing framework, common practice in the war years, eliminating the danger of flying glass fragments from shell or bomb blasts, but of no use against shrapnel and splinters. Of the two parts of today's conservatory, the left-hand side serves as a communal dining room for guests and staff alike. In wartime this was the Music and Recreation Room. Debates were a regular feature in this room, but military associated topics were strictly taboo with the exception of:

> . . . a hardy annual on the progress of the war. The voting on this was generally more instructive than the speeches . . .

A debate held on 17th December 1916, with an audience of 200 saw the motion carried that the war would be over by August of 1917. A week later, on the 24th, the house debated "Industrial Conscription" with regard to putting munitions' workers into khaki on soldiers pay. Its outcome, is unknown. On 2nd February 1916, another "In Support of Women's Suffrage" was heavily defeated by an obviously chauvinistic house. Other subjects recorded as being debated were: "The Economic Position of Women"; "Nationalisation of Railways"; "The Drink Problem"; "The Ethics of Scrounging" and "Ireland". Tubby remarks on one held in mid November 1917:

> A debate most interesting, both in its matter and its spirit, was on "The Colour Problem In The Empire", at which two British West Indian

sergeants made excellent speeches in English to an audience largely composed of Aussies and Canadians.

Any knowledge or understanding of the debate subject matter was not a necessity as sometimes the only criteria required was to have been press-ganged by the padre in the first place. As John H. Nicholson had discovered when in 1919 he wrote:

One of the jolliest feelings I know is to find that you haven't utterly forgotten how to do something that you've not done for years. There's nothing like a debate for shaking off mental cramp. To an old hand, condemned for years to the silence of the ranks or the boredom of shouting phrases which you mayn't vary by a hairs breadth, it is almost a fierce joy. There's a moment of horrid trembling at the knee when you first rise, and then you plunge headlong. Happy is he who, after a few fumbling sentences, falls unconsciously into his stride, and dear to his heart is the applause with which a generous audience rewards the effort, however footling.

My excuse for the following story must be that, if I had the wit to do it justice, it holds an element of humour. It was not of set purpose that I found myself pledged to stop a gap. I had been gazing absent-mindedly at the announcement of a debate, on which the opposers name had been newly erased — even debates must yield to the necessities of war. Suddenly I felt a pressure on my arm, kindly, persuasive, but infinitely compelling. Someone suggested — Oh! so tactfully — that I was exactly the person he was in search of, and hinted that I might save a difficult situation. It's horribly "intriguing" to be wanted as an individual and not as "one other ranks". There's a subtle flattery about it which scatters objections and modesties, like the paving stones of the Grande Place before the snub and solid nose of an 8 inch AP. Of course, I yielded. Can you show me a man who didn't?

Two days later, as I crawled self consciously through the ever open door, I'd have given a weeks pay to get out of it. My head was spinning like a top; my knees were a striking illustration of the "make and break" action of the armature of a Service "buzzer". Thoughts I had none.

It consoled me a little to find that the debate was in the open air. The Chairman's "Order! Order!" produced a horrid silence. My opponent, calm, confident, persuasive, piled up argument upon argument. My brain reeled. I covered an old envelope with frenzied jottings in a vain attempt at coherence. All too soon he sat down, smothered in applause. I heard my own name. I rose clutching the arm of my chair.

The imps that had taken possession of me did a war dance on my brain — a crew of merry rebels. I swallowed vigorously — and plunged. I shall never know what I said. My opponent afterwards compared by effusion to "a seance by Mrs Besant". I don't know whether that was meant as a compliment or a protest. The war dance stopped, and I sat down. The rest of the evening is indistinct. I have a vision of a hundred men, at a word of command from the chairman, flocking over to my side of the House, whether with intent to mob me, or to give me much needed support, I could hardly say.

I reached home safely. Next day people came and asked to borrow books about it. I assured them that for years I'd read nothing but "London Opinion" or at best "John Bull". They looked a little hurt. I hope I was nice to them. They wouldn't tell me what I had said. Perhaps for the honour of the House I should add a word of explanation. I had not tasted that evening of the waters of forgetfulness, but the night before I had unexpectedly been treated to a double dose of T.A.B.

Besides debates many lectures, delivered by both officers and men, were held. Town Planning, Housing Problems, Returning to Civilian Employment, being a few of the topics covered. On one occasion Tubby noted an unexpected indication of appreciation, at the time, giving him a little concern as to its consequence:

Such enterprises, again, have their pitfalls, and I remember my qualms at one of these meetings when a man I knew to be bitter got up in question time. He said, however, "I like the Army even less than most of you here" (awkward pause) "but I can't go away tonight without telling the officer that it has made all the difference in my outlook from henceforth to see he is ready to come here at the end of his day's work and put in an hour or so helping us to understand rightly things we have so much at heart."

Musical evenings were a regular feature in the conservatory with large numbers of men singing along to popular songs played on the piano. Tubby was always more than eager to participate in these "sing-songs", and he was favoured as a soloist with a surprisingly deep singing voice and repertoire of many comic songs. He said that on many a night the strains of *Goodbye-ee* reverberated throughout the House. Standing ever open at *It's a Long Way to Tipperary* on the piano today, the music and song book contains all those popular favourites. This was not the only type of music played as classical evenings and operatic arias were often arranged and always well attended.

Standing on top of the piano today is a gift, manufactured by a local coppersmith to commemorate the 75th anniversary of the Armistice in 1993. Known as the "Peace Pigeon" this hand-crafted bird, standing approximately 16-inches high, is made from bullet-heads, cases, and copper driving-bands of shells found in the salient.

On the wall to the left of the piano hangs the F. Matania print *Goodbye Old Man*. Commissioned by the Blue Cross in 1916, to raise money for the relief of suffering among war horses, it depicts a soldier of the Field Artillery cradling his badly wounded horse's head in his arms while the limbers continue along the shell-pocked road. Sub-titled *An Incident on the road to a Battery position in Southern Flanders*, and beneath it the poem:

## THE SOLDIER'S KISS

Only a dying horse! Pull off the gear,
And slip the needless bit from frothing jaws,
Drag it aside, there leave the roadway clear —
The battery thunders on with scarce a pause.

Prone by the shell-swept highway there it lies
With quivering limbs, as fast the life tide fails,
Dark films are closing o'er the faithful eyes
That mutely plead for aid where none avails.

Onward the battery rolls, but one there speeds,
Heedless of comrades voice or bursting shell,
Back to the wounded friend who lonely bleeds
Beside the stony highway where it fell.

Only a dying horse! He swiftly kneels,
Lifts the limp head and hears the shivering sigh
Kisses his friend, while down his cheek there steals
Sweet pity's tear; "Goodbye, old man, goodbye".

No honours wait him, medal, badge or star,
Though scarce could war a kindlier deed unfold;
He bears within his breast, more precious far
Beyond the gilt of Kings, a heart of gold.

*Henry Chappel*

It is said that the famous music-hall duo Flanagen and Allen first met and performed together in this room. After the war they went on to become internationally famous and formed "The Crazy Gang". Story has it that Bud Flanagen selected his stage name from that of his detested sergeant.

In the first year of occupancy, this room, and thereafter the Concert Hall, was set aside for what was to become an annual event, The Talbot House, Children's Christmas Party. These annual parties were a source of great joy to Tubby and those who assisted him, he recalled:

... on three occasions we feted them with incredible energy. Their great day was always December 6th, the Feast of St. Nicholas, on the eve of which the carrot is well and truly laid at the foot of the chimney to win the favour of his donkey at the conclusion of its precipitate downward career. Our parties took a prodigious amount of organising, and for weeks beforehand both the AMFO and the post corporal had their endurance greatly strained. Our first fête nearly broke down at the outset, for on arrival of the school I approached a dismal little boy, and asked him in French what he would like to play, to which he responded with a sad philosophy: "Belgian children have forgotten their games". Sure enough, an attempt at "hunt the slipper" was a miserable failure; but the happy inspiration of an apple, smeared with ration jam, and dependent on a string, between our pensive philosopher and a rival, both blindfold, quickly attained international celebrity. Five hundred cups of tea, after they were made, proved a novelty not so palatable; but the memory of this false step was drowned in Fry's Cocoa, brewed in supplementary buckets. After this, a Pathe film of a real Belgian pre-war fête brought the schoolmaster to his feet with a speech more eloquent than intelligible.

Jeanne Battheu fondly remembers this first Christmas Party:

I visited Talbot House for the first time in 1916. We were allowed to go there, but our father was always with us. We were made very welcome. Tubby told my father that we should come to Talbot House at Easter and on St. Nicholas Day. We were always given a box of toffees ... we were really spoiled. There was a big tree in the garden, and there were apples covered in jam hanging on the branches. We were blindfolded and then we had to try and grasp the apples with our teeth — no need to state that our faces were full of jam. We were also given a big piece of cheese, a box of toffees, toys, etc. We had a wonderful time.

A song sung at a party by Pettifer, Tubby's barman, went: "a girl so cross-eyed, that when she cried, her tears ran down her back" would have prompted strange thoughts in Belgian children's minds as to what their British counterparts were like. The last party, held on 1st January 1918, almost ended in tragedy when a bombing raid began shortly before the party ended. Luckily no one was harmed, the children were not the slightest bit worried by the raid, although the parents and staff were rather shaken. By the time news of this event reached England it had become somewhat distorted and caused:

... some melancholy Jacques in the House of Commons to floor a question as to the number of Belgian children who had been massacred at a party in Poperinghe by bombs dropped from an English aeroplane!

The wording of the letter of thanks indicates the bombing had not been severe enough to deserve mention:

Poperinghe, 8th Feb., 1918 ... Honoured Sirs, In the name of our 232 pupils we have the honour, from our whole hearts, to thank you for all of the toys which they have received from your generosity. With real gratitude they will remember the pleasant day which they spent and the kindness of their worthy benefactors. Very willingly do they pray the good God that He may spare the worthy officers from all dangers and fulfil all the desires of their goodness. Permit us to send you, honoured Sirs, the expression of our feelings of respect.

Signed: The Sisters of Boesinghe.

Lack of space prohibited attendance by the parents. In 1917, 232 children from one school alone were admitted. This was made possible during the late Spring of 1917 when VIII Corps, in preparation for the Battle of Messines, arrived in Poperinghe. Adjoining the house were a number of large out-houses and men of the Corps, converted the nearest one into what became the "Concert Hall". Prior to this conversion large gatherings from the house met at one of the concert venues in the town or in the nearby villages.

**The Concert Hall**. Every Division had its own "Concert Party" composed of men from the regiments within the Division whose sole responsibility was to provide entertainment for those men in camps and towns behind the lines. Many of the performers had been household names in "civvy street" and were extremely popular with the troops. In one of his earliest letters from Poperinghe Tubby said that he was looking forward to seeing "Box and Cox" performed at "The Fancies" on Christmas Eve 1915 by men of the Royal Army Veterinary Corps, the Mobile Vets. He was a regular visitor to "The Fancies", a large hopstore near the railway station. On one occasion, watching the 6th Division's "A Great Divisional Show", he said:

. . . justly celebrated for Fred Chandler's tenor voice, Dick Home's (QWR Transport Section)

"Rogerum" (a coon song version of the Parable of Dives and Lazarus, with a magnificently onomatopoeic chorus, which lifted the Sixth Division along over many miles of mud) . . . They lent us their hall on Sunday nights, where in front of a drop scene painfully reminiscent of the Canal Bank in November, Neville preached the Gospel of Faith and Freedom.

"Rogerum", the marching song of the Queen's Westminster Rifles, was special to him. In December 1915, Clayton heard 35 survivors of the regiment singing it one night as they returned to their billet next-door to Talbot House after a harrowing spell in the trenches. From then on he forbade the lyrics to be sung by any other unit and, in later years, extended this to the Boy Scouts and even his beloved Boys' Clubs.

Ronald H. Brewster, Queen's Westminster Rifles recalled:

The Old House has shut for the night, the last straggler has been ejected, the last penny has been taken at the canteen for a hurried cup of tea, but as yet no move has been made to turn out the lights on the ground floor. Visitors are expected. By special permission two Companies of Infantry billeted nearby are coming in for a late concert. In the hop-loft across the garden the Sunday furnishings have been carefully stored away and the stage has been set with old sheets of canvas to form wings and back cloth. The tramp of marching men is heard and the stirring marching song "O Rogerum" reverberates through silent Pop; our guests have arrived. Crowding in with cheery badinage to all and sundry they file through the House and take their seats in the hop-loft as keenly interested as if they were in the pit of their local theatre at home. The concert begins, but not before a dark and secret conference between Tubby and the musical director has taken place to decide how some half a dozen scratch turns collected in the course of the day by the former are to be sandwiched into an already complete programme. Now all is arranged and Tubby steps onto the platform to open the proceedings with a cheery word to the troops. He meets with a certain amount of good-natured heckling but gives as good as he gets. Tonight we are very fortunate. Some of the 55th Divisional Concert Party are with us and some of the Divisional Band, not to mention two dear old souls from a Labour Battalion who are going to do their best. The pianist is now heard at work playing popular songs and the full-throated response from the audience sets the keynote for the whole evening's proceedings. Who is the comedian just taking his applause? Why, Du Calion, the well known music hall artist who does and says such clever and alarming things whilst balanced at the top of a long ladder. True, the height of the hop-loft forbids the use of his ladder, but what of that? — the troops don't expect to find a music hall artist of his eminence playing for their pleasure in a spot like this. A quartet of brass instruments has just played some popular opera airs, which please all mightily; an aged Permanent Base man (who earns his living in peace-time making and selling woollen flowers at fairs and on race courses) has obliged with "She's the pride of Liscarrell, is sweet Katie O'Farrell" and has made the whole room sing the chorus with him in true sentimental fashion; a tenor and an elocutionist have charmed us; whilst last but not least Tubby has sung "The Mishipmite" and has had everybody singing a beat behind him in the lugubrious lines which refer to the "Lowland Sea". The concert is over and the Commanding Officer has made a speech of thanks, the troops have given three cheers for the artists and away they march to their billets with "Rogerum" helping them along. The staff lock up and retire to rest hoping the concert will however slightly, have helped their comrades to face still cheerfully the horrors and rigours of the Ypres Salient.

Of a particularly memorable performance Tubby was to comment:

One Summer day, in 1917, a concert of the easiest kind was being held in the then newly opened hall of Talbot House in Poperinghe. The hall had been made by breaking through the wall into a farther hop-loft with a stronger floor, and a wooden staircase led from the garden to the hole in the wall, secured by an adapted door. This hall came to a bad end, for it was struck by two shells in quick succession in 1918. On the day of which I am thinking, the sing-song somewhat lagged . . . when I had almost reached the point of putting myself on, an unknown gunner entered the hall, and I asked him whether he could sing. He gave me an odd look; and shrugging his shoulders, passed towards the platform. On the platform were a few pieces of scenery, among which he disappeared. A moment later he came back in full view upon the stage, and the universal genius at the piano struck up a lively tune.

The gunner now removed his tunic, and took from the pocket a toothbrush, rag and polish tin, and sat himself cross legged on the one stage chair. By this time the piano had died away completely, and the audience was watching and expecting the preliminary patter of a comic song. What happened was far different. A humming began to come from between the man's lips as he polished his buttons. The tune gradually took shape, most exquisitely rendered. When the air had taken hold of our minds, it reappeared clothed in words, and these are the words he sang:

"There was no one like 'im, 'Orse or Foot,
Nor any 'o the Guns I knew;
An' because it was so, why, o' course 'e went an'
   died,
Which is just what the best men do."

By the time the first verse was sung we were spellbound. We knew that we were in the presence of a great artist. Many such had at various times found their way to Talbot House, but none so strangely as this unknown man. There were whispers of identification, but the anonymity was not withdrawn. Then he proceeded to the verse:

"We fought 'bout a dog — last week it were —
No more than a round or two
But I strook 'im cruel 'ard, an' I wish I 'adn't now,
Which is just what a man can't do.

'E was all that I 'ad in the way of a friend,
An' I've to find one new;
But I'd give my pay an' stripe to get the beggar
   back,
Which it's just too late to do!

So it's knock out your pipes an' follow me!
An' it's finish up your swipes an' follow me!
Oh 'ark to the fifes a-crawlin'!
Follow me — follow me 'ome!"

By this time we had realised something more. This man was a great artist, yes. But this thing was not art in the sense of sudden enrichment of an entertainment by mere skill. This man was singing his soul. There had been losses in his battery, and he had come down with Kipling's immortal song in his mind and he had found a concert which he could convert into a congregation with whose aid he might offer that amazing requiem.

"Take 'im away! 'E's gone where the best men go.
Take 'im away! An' the gun wheels turnin' slow.
Take 'im away! There's more from the place 'e come
Take 'im away! With the limber an' the drum.
For it's 'Three rounds blank' 'an follow me,
An' it's 'Thirteen rank' 'an follow me;
Oh, passin' the love o' women
Follow me — follow me 'ome!"

As he finished there was absolute silence, the one possible tribute. The gunner rose, slipped on his tunic and came down the hall. Leaving the concert to look after itself, I pursued him. I did not ask him who he was ... I only tried to thank him, as I would thank him now once more. I have never known a man's soul thus shining through his art. He was in no mood for talking, and quickly disappeared into the night.

By the winter of 1917 Talbot House had its own concert party and band under the direction of Charles Wilmott, 70th Labour Company who, later in civilian life, became manager of the Brixton Theatre of Varieties in London. The group constructed a stage set consisting of wings and a backcloth out of sheets of canvas on which scenes were painted. The group performed comic detective stories and "grotesque parodies in which

Tubby put up a good show". Of the Talbot House Concert Party, 1917-18, he said:

We had a dramatic party of our very own, which acted with amazing eclat, "Detective Keen" and similar dramas, complete to the last revolver and the dumbest telephone. As a Spring pantomime, we rose to "The Critic", in which I doubled the parts of the Beefeater and Tilburina, an arrangement at which Sheridan would have shuddered.

An account of one of the performances given by the Talbot House concert party relates to its visit to Ypres in 1918:

On March 19th we even gave a performance in the YMCA just inside the Lille Gate at Ypres, being (I think) the only theatrical party that accomplished this. The New Zealanders there paid courteous attention for a while, but the noble work of the master wit might have found no purchase on their Caledonian souls, had not the whispering whine of several gas-shells without caused the heroine suddenly to dart into the wings, reappearing thence with a "boxspirator" at the ready. This quite broke the ice, and all went merrily henceforth. The next day, I believe, a gas-shell pitched on the billiard-table there, and a few days later the hut itself was wrecked. Even as we spoke the mocking lines, "England's fate, like a clipped guinea, trembles in the scales", the fact indeed was so.

Not averse to advertising the group's services Tubby produced the following notice:

Anyone who thinks that their unit would enjoy a visit from our Concert Party, or a performance of our pantomime or "Box and Cox", or "Detective Keen", should get in touch with either QMS Johnson (8th Corps Sigs.), or Sergeant Evans (Delousing Station), or Pte. Wilmot, or myself here in the House. The transport can be arranged, we can gladly bring any of these shows to you, but cannot for the present use our Concert Hall here, as closely packed audiences in the town are for the time taboo.

The notice in the Conservatory *Come Into The Garden and forget about the War* was put up in May 1916 and:

almost the first acceptance of the invitation was intimated by the arrival of a 5.9 which blew sideways into the House, mortally wounding a Canadian who had come in with his brother. In point of fact this was the only fatal casualty within the House.

In the same month Tubby was evacuated to a hospital at Boulogne, suffering from a bout of recurrent malaria, where he would stay until mid August of that year. During Tubby's absence the House was run by Neville Talbot who, mentioning the 5.9, wrote, on May 29th:

Dear Tubby, The Staff will have to go sooner or later, but I am fighting for Godley and Kirklan. We had a beastly shelling yesterday (Sunday). I was up at Elverdinghe for HA. A high explosive landed in the garden just opposite men's latrines, house spattered — a Canadian mortally wounded in hall — a bit driven through four folding doors and through window on street. Hambling had the wind up — he has gone on leave . . . Bless You. Ever Yours. N.S. Talbot.

Added to this letter is a pencilled note made by Tubby:

A letter from Neville Talbot, who took charge while I was in hospital in May, 1916. The 5.9 referred to landed in the garden and blew through the House, mortally wounding a Canadian who had come in with his brother to write a joint letter home. "Godley" is ex-Sergt. Godley.

The damage caused by this shell he also referred to:

I was found asleep in my chair. This time it was a Dorset subaltern who woke me, his face alive with humour. He prophesied in rapid succession a number of inevitable consequences — I should be shot at dawn, and the Church would be disestablished; the Corps Commander was without, asking for me; the Kaiser had ordered breakfast, and so on. I sat up and looked about me. "As you see," I said, "at least I have been sleeping in the line of fire." And I pointed to the holes in the old door leading to the conservatory, and in the window opening on the narrow street. A piece of shrapnel had recently passed through the room, and given it an element of ventilation which the Belgian architect had never intended it to possess.

When Tubby and Neville Talbot took over the House the garden was fairly well kept, but Tubby was too preoccupied with other matters to give it much attention until the Spring of 1916 when he decided:

March 20th, 1916 . . . Meanwhile the garden looms large in my projects — a badminton court in the kitchen garden for officers and the repainting of the summer house for their delectation; and weeding and pruning everywhere . . . The weather is perfect and the wall fruit trees and roses need a lot of wisdom that is beyond me. The Band is coming into the garden as soon as we have got it straight, every afternoon more or less, so we shall be cheerier than ever . . . Now I must go and tackle the garden, which I think and hope is going to be not only a great delight to my guests, but also a great source of recreation for me.

Shortly after he was "loaned" the services of a Lance Corporal from a nearby Labour Battalion whom he employed for many weeks as a full time gardener.
Visiting Talbot House was not without its dangers:

During the varying fortunes of the salient, shells crossed and recrossed the roof from three points of the compass at least. Bombs landed in the garden, in the street, in the Magazin next door. One bright afternoon in the summer of 1917, when there were close on 700 men in the House and garden, a big naval shell blew the house next door into a cocked hat, but only slightly wounded a man on our verandah. I do not comment on this, but I have heard older soldiers than I ever want to be say what they thought about it.

and:

Monday, August 6th 1917 . . . We had a narrow shave for the House on Monday last about 7p.m. when a 9.5 landed in the little house next door, and blew it to bits. Fortunately the folk who live there were out, or they would have lived there no longer. Several chunks came into the Library wall, two boys were blown out of hammocks, one other was slightly wounded, about 50 lying about in the garden were rudely awakened, the place filled with smoke and plaster; but by a miracle no serious damage was done. Another five yards higher on a 15 mile flight, and TH would have gone west with a hundred casualties at best. Laus Deo!

For many years, land to the rear of the garden wall bore a reminder of early 1915 shellfire:

. . . a brace had landed in the orchard at the back of what was afterwards Talbot House. One of these immigrants had created a pond, in which its brother, a dud, was committed to rest in a frivolous funeral.

The garden was a popular place of relaxation where the men could lounge peacefully on the lawn — Tubby called them "Khaki Basking Lizards" — sit and read, stand and talk, or enjoy personal solitude and a moment's reflection. One soldier, while sitting peacefully, and appearing to be half asleep, was approached by Tubby who asked him if there was anything he needed. His reply went something like:

I'm perfectly fine sitting here thinking of home. Listening to the two washer women next door, the sound of their chattering, is just like that of my mother and our neighbour when they do the same on wash day.

It was also possible to enjoy a game of draughts or chess, as related by another "How Not To Win The War" scenario:

Scene 1. Halfway down the garden. Two chairs and garden table; with tin board and draughtsmen thereon, also a rubbish box in foreground. Enter two gunners with mugs of tea and paper bag of fruit. One gunner upsets draughtsmen on to grass, and deposits mug on table. The other amends this procedure by seating himself on the ground, turning the half-full rubbish box upside down, and placing his mug thereon. Finally enter Padre: tableau vivant.

Today, the thatched summer house with its white painted verandah is no longer to be seen to the left-hand side of the central mound. And the dilapidated out-buildings where the Carpenter's Bench was discovered have been replaced by the Garden House accommodation building. Gone too from the:

... left-hand corner of the lawn is the "Aviary" in which Neville Talbot proposed his huge charger "Jumbo" should "play the part of a large canary" on a visit in 1916.

The dovecote on the garden mound is an exact replica of the one that stood fast here throughout the war. When the original eventually fell into disrepair it was replaced by an adequate, but less ornate, substitute which lasted for many years before being destroyed by storms in 1995.

A manhole covering to the immediate right of the lawn, just outside of the House, was the entrance to what were the cellars of a hop-store that stood on or near this spot many years before the war and which served as:

... a frankly inadequate "funk-hole" when enemy planes were bombing over Poperinghe.

In later years a 300-foot deep artesian well was sunk next to this entrance serving the then much improved bath "Pavilion" which catered to the needs of the post-war visitors to Talbot House. The "Pavilion", funded by Major Paul Slessor with much of his own money, was built in 1930, at the suggestion of the War Graves Commission, and renamed "The Slessorium". For a bath-house it was not only very large, but caused many problems in its construction. The plans were drawn up by British architects using imperial measurements but the Belgian contractors used metric when building it. The problems came to light only when the particularly large bore plumbing was queried. Women could not enter if a man was showering, and vice-versa, as there were no shower curtains. There was no lock on the door of the building either. The original small boiler shed facility for the old "Bath House" still stands alongside the Slessorium which, having itself fallen into disrepair, was extensively renovated, and is today called the Visitor Centre, used mainly for visitor gatherings, meetings and small exhibitions.

# CHAPTER
# FIVE

# All Rank Abandon

. . . across the hall came the sound of voices
and a piano, but I wanted to investigate
the stairway, so miraculously reminding
me of home

*Douglas Legg*


A steep narrow staircase leads to the first floor, flanked
on one side by a wooden banister and on the other a wall
hung with Barclay Baron water-colours depicting scenes
within the house during the Great War together with Eric
Kennington's *Grave of Man*.

On the landing halfway up these stairs stands the
"Cadenza Chimes", used to summon worshippers to the
Chapel. They were thought to be made of four
large-calibre shell-bases until, in September 1998, they
were discovered to be purpose-built. The four discs,
when struck in a certain order, sound identical to that of
a Westminster clock chimes.

The alcove immediately behind the Cadenza Chimes
was used to house a nativity crib at Christmas time
during the war. The first one burnt before it could be
installed, when a candle set it alight. In 1916 Corporal

Stagg fashioned one from a cardboard box, with figures purchased from a toy shop in Dunkirk. Today the alcove holds a wooden statuette of St. Peter, donated by Czech soldiers who salvaged it from a ruined church in Ghyvelde in northern France.

On the right at the top of the stairs is a notice stating *No Amy Robstart stunts down these stairs, by request, P.B.C.* It refers to the death of Amy Robstart, Countess of Leicester alleged to have been the wife of the adulterous lover of Queen Elizabeth I, found dead at the foot of a flight of stairs. Another sign, *Down these stairs in signal phial*, speaks for itself.

On one wall of the landing is a copy of Eric Kennington's sketch of T. E. Lawrence and on the wall facing the stairs is a water colour entitled *Belgian Peasants praying over the Souls of the Dead*. Painted in 1916, it was presented to the house by H.R.H. Prince of Wales whilst he was on the staff of XIV Corps in Poperinghe.

A mirror to the right serves to help read the letter alongside from an Argyll and Sutherland Highlander who left behind a testimonial in March 1918. Written backwards, it reads:

Flanders. Twelveth. Marck (sic) Eighteen. To the Officer in charge of Talbot House.
SIR,
On my first visit to "Talbot House" to-day I was almost amazed at the splendid arrangements made to provide what I honestly think it is, a "Home from Home", and I congratulate you and your staff on

the completeness of the comforts provided for the Soldiers. I may add that during the years Sixteen and Seventeen I visited many so-called Soldiers Homes or Huts both in France and Flanders but this splendidly equipted (sic) House stands unequalled. May God give you strength and grace to "Carry-on."

I am Respectfully, Pte. McNaught, A and S. Hrs., Attd. Ninty (sic) Seventh Bde. H.Q., "Cinema", B.E.F., Flanders.

On the first floor there were once five bedrooms and a dressing room. Today there are four individually named rooms, the fifth now a bathroom. The latter was originally a long room divided in two by a wooden partition and a wardrobe described by a Douglas Legg as:

Upstairs on the first floor I found a tiny room, lined with books and even a cursory glance showed me that they were books to read — the sort of book I had been starving for for months. I chose one from the shelves, but had scarcely settled myself when closing time arrived.

This library, kept in the larger one of the divided rooms, held in excess of 2,000 books, most of which are now kept in the house archives.

Donald Cox of the London Rifle Brigade resorted to verse in his description of it:

Behold! all ye who seek companions fair
For half a day, a day, perhaps a week,
Enter and take your choice, for here you find
The very book (or books) your soul doth seek.
Love you far shores? here's tales of distant lands;
Or incident? here's history to your hands.
Or do you love the men who nobly live?
Biographies shall satisfaction give;
Fiction, to lose yourself a quiet hour;
Training to give your body grace and power;
Poetry, with her poppied embrace;
Religion, to give your spirit grace;
Oh! all you men who recreation seek
Come, choose your boon companion for a week.

Tubby's own description is less poetical:

To imagine Talbot House library you must conceive
of a very large cupboard, or a very small room,
literally so crammed with books that the librarian
himself could sometimes scarcely enter.

Although he also chose to write:

"I never did," murmured the library, set with a shoe
horn into one small room, "there are men coming
constantly to me and asking for all sorts and kinds
of books ... I am here to teach the Church that
men have minds, and that those minds are
hungering and thirsting. Men cannot really lift their
hearts to God unless their minds are also lifted up.

Their mental processes may be peculiar; their duties are no 'battle of the books'; but I stand here to prove that Talbot House encourages their minds to operate. Our Lord was not alarmed by men with minds. He never trusted cleverness per se; but He had every use for honest thinking".

A Major G. Brimley-Bowes, noted:

. . . if we thirsted for literature, the library (when it was not crowded out) bade us come and choose, but not forget to inscribe in the "Lent not Lost" book.

And Tubby again:

To borrow one of these books you left your Army cap in pawn, and took the volume to any part of the House or garden where you spied a chair or a corner unappropriated.

When a man borrowed a book he would leave his Army cap as a "ticket", retrieving it on returning the book. In the case of officers the "Lent not Lost" system was used. The book title was recorded with the borrower's name and signature. Every book and magazine was rubber-stamped with either "Confined to the Library", "Little Talbot House, Ypres" or "Not to be Scrounged".

Many were not returned, proof evident when the secretary of the Talbot House Association, visiting a

Paris flea market in 1992, came across a number of books and magazines stamped *Not To Be Scrounged*. These were bought for the house. After the war, particularly during the 1930's, a number of books were returned from as far afield as Canada and New Zealand.

Magazines such as "Nash", "Punch", the "Spectator", and "Bystander" were all to be found in the library as were copies of "The Wipers Times", the trench newspaper of the Sherwood Foresters; one story in the latter was said to be contributed by Tubby:

Reflections on being lost in Ypres at 3a.m.

I wish I had been more studious as a youth. Then I should not have neglected the subjects I disliked. Then I should not have failed to cultivate the sense of geography. And thus I should not have contrived to lose myself so often in Ypres in the small hours of winter mornings.

Lost in Ypres, it is an eerie experience. Not a soul to be seen not a voice to be heard. Only far out on the road to Hooge, the quick impulsive rattle of the British machine guns answers the slower more calculating throbbing of the Hun variety. If a man would understand what hate means, let him wander along the Menin Road in the evening, and then let him find some poet, or pioneer, or artilleryman to express what he feels concerning the Hun operator in that concrete, machine-gun redoubt.

Lost in Ypres at night: in the daytime it is a difficult feat to accomplish. Transports and troops pass and re-pass along the ruined streets. From almost every aspect, through gigantic holes torn in the intervening walls, the rugged spikes of the ruined cathedral town mark the centre of the town. From time to time, too, the heavy thud of a "crump" (like some old and portly body falling through a too frail chair with a crash to the floor), is an unerring guide to the main square.

But at night all is different. The town is well-nigh deserted. All its inhabitants, like moles, have come out at dusk and have gone, pioneers and engineers, to their work in the line. Night after night they pass through dangerous ways to more dangerous work. Lightly singing some catchy chorus they move to and fro across the open road, in front of the firing line, or hovering like black ghosts about the communication trenches, as if there was no such thing as war. The whole scene lights up in quick succession round the semi-circle of the salient as the cold relentless star-shells sail up into the sky. Here and there a "grouser" airs his views, but receives little sympathy, for the men are bent on their work and do it with a will.

All this while however, I have been standing lost in Ypres. I cannot steer by the star-shells, for they seem to be on every side. And at night, too, the jagged spires of the cathedral are reduplicated by the remains of buildings all over the city. Like the fingers of ghosts they seem to point importunately to heaven, crying for vengeance. It is a city of ghosts, the city of the dead. For it and with it the sons of three nations have suffered and died. Yet within that city, not many days ago, a little maid of Flanders was found playing. That is an omen. Ypres has died but shall live again. Her name in the past was linked with Kings; but tomorrow she will have a nobler fame. Men will speak of her as the home of the British soldier who lives in her mighty rampart caverns or in the many cellars of her mansions. And even when the busy hum of everyday life shall have resumed its sway in future days, still there will be heard in ghostly echo the muffled rumbling of the transport and the rhythmic tread of soldiers' feet.

By "The Padre"

**The bathroom** today carries a sign stating: *This Is A Library, Not A Dormitory*. Above it is a Barclay Baron watercolour of the library as it was during the war. The librarian in the painting is probably Lance-Corporal George Trower, who held the post from 1917-18:

Church Shop
Cpl. Trower, the Librarian has also charge of the Church Shop. This was started some time ago for the use of padres. But as a large number of men wish to purchase Bibles, religious books etc., they

can gladly have the run of the shop on application to him.

**The Dunkirk Room**, one of two large rooms immediately opposite the bathroom was named in remembrance of the B.E.F. evacuation from the beaches of Dunkirk, following the German invasion of France and Belgium in May 1940.

During those dark days Poperinghe once again played an important part for the British Army when over 250,000 men were amassed in the town on their way to the coast.

Apart from the title the only reminder of Dunkirk is a watercolour by C. Dick, entitled *Rearguard action on the Dunkirk approaches. May 26th 1940. Argyll and Sutherland Highlanders* showing two machine guns firing at the advancing German infantry. During the war the Dunkirk Room served a variety of functions. At one time, alternating as Chaplain's Room, it was also used as the Writing Room with tables and chairs, pens, paper, ink and envelopes available for the men to sit and write letters to families and friends. It was primarily an officers' room equipped with a miniature billiard table where "fifty-up" was constantly played, complete with a sign, to prevent tearing the cloth, claiming *The Good Player Chalks His Cue Before He Plays; The Bad Player After*:

Here, round the trestle-tables, bedecked as well as they might be with a bowl or two of flowers, men sat and wrote illimitably, or stood and waited their

turn. To watch the twenty lucky ones at work was a first hand insight into the varieties of educational standards which still exist in England. Here was the accomplished penman lolling at his ease and flinging fireworks of phrases into every paragraph. Here also was the great dumb son of the soil squaring his elbows to a task more exacting and unusual than any which the war called upon him to perform.
P.B. Clayton.

One of the duties of the librarian was to ensure that the ink-pots were full, adequate stationery was available, and that the pens were serviceable. Of the latter Tubby comments:

One common failing of the British race when engaged in the agonies of composition is to lean all too sternly upon the comparatively frail instrument which conveys their thoughts to paper. The result is pitiful and disastrous, and the ink flies everywhere. I doubt if the total output of letters that day was within a hundred of the day preceding.

And, also on pens:

Bother! who was this coming in? An officer of some sort! I thought a padre ran the show. What is this chap? A Northumberland Fusilier captain. Have we got to stand up? No! He says he's been sent round that floor by the padre to see if the nibs are up to scratch! One fellow at the table says that's just what his is, and indents on the captain for a new one. Queer place this. Mem. Must be looked into more closely tomorrow night. Mem. Wash out that estaminet crawl. That captain with the nibs was a bit of a nib himself. Wish he was in our Batt.

Seating was always at a premium, and it was often difficult to find somewhere to sit. Tubby posted a notice:

How not to win the war.

Scene 2: The first floor writing room. Both windows tightly closed. Various literary gentlemen busily engaged in calligraphy.

Enter two RAMC representatives, afraid of too generous a supply of fresh air on the balcony. Each carries three magazines, and two books from the library. These they deposit among the inkpots, pens and blotting paper, and proceed to absorb in a slow but expansive manner. Enter more persons desiring to write letters. (Curtain.)

The "Writing Room" or "Dunkirk Room" as it is now was to the immediate right of its present position and linked internally by a door to what later became, and is still known as the Chaplain's room.
**The Chaplain's Room** has its original sign above the door, *All rank abandon, ye who enter here. Chaplain's Room*.

A centre panel, added 26th August 1931, by ex Staff Officer Alan Colthurst, explains:

The innkeeper's first parlour was on the ground-floor, now the steward's private room. When this became the tea-bar in 1916, he moved his room up here using the General's bedroom for his kip . . . In 1917 this room became a little room for tea and quiet writing: while the innkeeper moved next door so as to keep an eye on the Canadian lounge. All the team-workers helping with the house knew this room best of all, next to the Chapel: and strangers ceased their shyness, once inside.

It was to this room that the downstairs sign *Come upstairs and risk meeting the Padre* related. Rank was non-existent, men talked to one another as equals, breaking down barriers between the social classes. Friendships were forged in this room and meetings took place that under any other circumstances simply would not have happened.

I remember, for instance, one afternoon on which the tea party (there generally was one) comprised a General, a staff captain, a second lieutenant, and a Canadian private. After all why not? There was, moreover, always a fair percentage of temporary officers who had friends not commissioned whom they longed to meet. The padre's meretricious pips seemed in such cases to provide an excellent chaperonage. Yet further, who knows what may be behind the private's uniform? I mind me of another afternoon when a St. John's undergraduate, for duration a wireless operator with artillery, sat chatting away. A knock, and the door opened timidly to admit a middle-aged RFA driver, who looked chiefly like one in search of a five-franc loan. I asked (I hope courteously) what he wanted, whereupon he replied: "I could only find a small Cambridge manual on palaeolithic man in the library. Have you anything less elementary?" I glanced sideways at the wireless boy and saw that my astonishment was nothing to his. "Excuse me, sir," he broke in, addressing the driver, "but surely I used to come to your lectures at College." "Possibly," replied the driver, "mules are still my speciality".

Alan G. Colthurst, 235 Brigade Royal Field Artillery, was privy to a number of Tubby's informal gatherings:

Talbot House was a unique experience for this was the only place in the war zone where officers and men could meet on a social footing. I arrived booted and spurred with red tabs on my uniform, a staff officer, and stood hesitant in the open doorway. I faced a room packed with laughing soldiers of every rank with Tubby dressed in blue blazer and shorts, who laughed loudest of all. At sight of me there was a hush and Tubby stopped talking — with his mouth wide open — then — "Good Lord — Come in Sir." I found my cap with

its red band seized and then thrown unceremoni-
ously under his bed, a place made for me beside a
corporal of signallers and a chuckling voice in my
ear saying "Now then sir, talk." I sat tongue tied,
but was soon chatting with the corporal as if he was
my best friend. Such was the magic of Tubby.

Tubby wrote of one of the gatherings held during
Easter 1917:

Our Easter Sunday supper was a merry meal to
which about ten, both officers and men, sat down.
These small and wisely mixed Sunday suppers had
become by this time a regular institution, the
founders of the feast being chiefly a Norfolk major,
Harry Jago of the Devons, and myself.

Jago was a great joy to us all at this anxious time;
indeed, it is impossible to imagine him anywhere at
any time without the same thing being truly said of
him. He had come in first as if by accident; and
from that time onwards leapt by sheer splendour of
character into a great place in our common life. I
remember well one afternoon when the Devons,
down from Passchendaele the night before,
announced their return visit by the visit of two
young West-Country lads, who arrived with a
present of books from a faithful sergeant. A few
minutes later they were at tea, when the door of my
room opened again to admit their major. Seeing
their awkwardness, nothing would content him but

that he should seat himself between them and draw them out both as their share in the past week's work and their Devonian lore.

On this occasion the conversation between these men went on far into the night with Tubby ending his account on a sombre note:

... later in the summer, the news came of the day when the whole battalion, colonel, 28 officers, and 552 non-commissioned officers and men, isolated and without hope of assistance, held onto their trenches north of the river, and fought to the last with unhesitating obedience to orders, we knew that all the trumpets had sounded for them on the other side.

Captain Leonard Browne, RAMC, who nicknamed Tubby "Boniface" wrote of his memories of the Chaplain's Room:

Many a time I have sat in that room of his at Talbot House and watched a succession of men coming in, many of them tired and jaded after a tramp from "Wipers". "My dear old man, how ripping to see you!" Boniface had the true spirit of hospitality which put the most awkward man at his ease, and made him feel that here was one who really cared nothing for a man's stripes but would be the same to all. Shy lads from Devon and Somerset, men from Northumberland and

Durham, awkward, but keen and intelligent, self possessed Londoners, men from Australia, Canada, and New Zealand, all fell under the same spell . . . and it was the power of an unselfish love for them which brought these men back to the House over and over again. I remember one hot Sunday afternoon in June while a lot of us were sitting at tea in the House, a great burly, red-haired Australian gunner arrived on a push-bike from Armentieres. He had only come to see the padre for a few minutes. As a matter of fact he had exactly half an hour, which he had to share with other people, but he went away with a light in his eyes which mirrored the feelings within.

and Lieutenant Burgon Bickersteth remembers:

August 1917. In the morning we went to Poperinghe by car and had lunch with Clayton at Talbot House. Talbot House is a wonderful institution. I had never seen it before, as it was only founded in December 1915, and I had not been in Poperinghe since that June. We had our meal with Clayton and three private soldiers — the first I had ever sat down to eat out here in uniform with soldiers.

Men would often come to Tubby for a private audience. It is said that at the close of such audiences a much calmer and happier man would emerge.

Using the first line of a poem by Lieutenant E. A. Mackintosh as a lead-in Tubby reminiscences:

Oh! my, I don't want to die. I've sat all through the night with a good officer sobbing with fear under the presentiment that the next journey would be his last. Private X was a man who from the first was always in trouble — really bad trouble, such as striking NCO's, etc. — and yet when there was any dangerous job on he was among the first to volunteer, and he ended his life in a gallant raid. Utterly undisciplined, intolerant of all authority, and yet eager for the job which he had joined the army to do, and for which he gave his life. In the dark of a dug-out, the fine old colonel admits that he never goes to sleep until he has said his evening hymn. Crouched in the shell hole, one man pulls out the Gospels and reads silently, until the others tell him to read aloud. Struggling back from the Menin Road, is a stretcher bearer alone with a wounded man. A gas-cloud overwhelms them, and the wounded man has lost his gas-mask. Yet in the morning light a mask is found upon his face, with the stretcher bearer stifling beside him. To ignore the reality of this inner besiegement, in which they were beset by every doubt and devil in hell, is to rob their accomplishment of its true virtue and their valour of its teaching power. During the war I was an innkeeper, and as such became the unheroic confidant of many customers. Few of those customers came home.

**The General's Room** earned its title by virtue of the fact that it was the only room with the luxury of a real bed with real sheets, not because a General slept there. For the sum of 5 francs, which included a late supper and breakfast, an officer just out of the line was more than happy to be accommodated in one of the eleven stretcher-beds with an army blanket to cover him. There was no extra charge for this room but the user was encouraged to make a suitable donation for the privilege, the money being put towards cigarettes and beverages for other ranks. The "donation" was never a deterrent, the room was in constant use.

Those were the days of simplicity; and I can see now officers waiting semi-somnolently in chairs until their luckier brethren got up for breakfast and the leave train, to play Box to their Cox, so that Rev. Mrs. Bouncer had a grateful though a sleepless task. The House was always what the Canadians called a "soft-drink" establishment, but no one resented this, lapping up tea or cocoa or bovril with thanksgiving. True, they were mostly infantry officers, who had learned such thankfulness in a rough school. One noticed, moreover, the meticulous care with which the old officer looked after the needs of his servant and his horse before his own. At no period of the war, I suppose, were the officers of any army up to our standard early in '16, when the flower of our amateurs stood side by side with those regulars who had survived both the hazards of war and the temptations of

91

tabs. The fact that the House was, financially considered, a gift from the officers to the men was characteristic of the unity of spirit which possessed them both.

The first two officers stayed over on 14th December 1915 and in excess of 1,000 men stayed overnight between then and 7th April 1916.

On the walls of the General's Room hang two prints. One, a copy of G. S. Frasers', 1935 painting *The Upper Room*, and the other, D.Y. Cameron, RA's *The Battlefield of Ypres*.

**The Berat Room**, used for accommodation during the war, as it is today, was named after Rene and Alida Berat, the first Belgian housekeepers who provided a warm welcome to the early "pilgrims" from 1929 until forced to leave by the Germans in 1941.

**The Canadian Lounge** was constructed in 1917 by men of the Newfoundland Regiment. Sited on the roof of the conservatory, its main support was a telegraph pole rammed through the roof and footed in the tiled floor below. Its walls were made of wire-mesh covered with roofing felt on the outside and cardboard on the inside. Access was provided by the two large windows on the first floor landing:

Housing about 70 men, it was here that chess, draughts, ping-pong and conversation flourished.

Today the only reminder of the room's original use is a photograph and a Barclay Baron watercolour, both showing a multi-beamed room with trestle-tables, chess and dart boards, chairs, and gramophone. During the summer of 1917 this extension provided Tubby with extra income by enabling him to accommodate more men overnight.

# CHAPTER
# SIX

# The Antechamber

Every Picture Tells A Story
*Proverb*.

In 1915 there were only three bedrooms and a large nursery on this second floor, with the space this large landing afforded being earmarked to serve as the Chapel:

Talbot House. Monday, Dec. 6th 1915 . . . and on Sunday morning at 11.15 the first Celebration in our Chapel (a big landing on the second floor). There is room for fifty or sixty, and I hope we shall have it full. Celebrations out here have nearly always to be regardless of the fasting rule, owing to exigencies of work.

Wednesday, Dec. 15th . . . On Sunday, our little Chapel was full for the Celebration at 11.15, and there is every promise of it being the centre of real work and worship among the men coming and going through here. It is work I more or less understand and does not involve any regimental red tape.

With Christmas 1915 fast approaching, Talbot House was to give the men a celebration with all the trappings of home. Carol sheets were ordered from England, then copied by officers so that their men in the trenches might also sing them, and a Christmas tree was set up in the recreation room on the ground floor. In a letter to his mother Tubby wrote:

What with singing and games of all sorts, I hope for a really happy Christmas for us all please God . . .

. . . The first Christmas in the House was a great success and enjoyed by all who attended during the day . . .

. . . Sunday, December 26th . . . The Chapel on the landing is simply splendid — everyone has put in time, taste and trouble to make it as perfect as possible. The only disadvantage is that it will only hold fifty at the outside. We hold Evensong there daily at 7.15, with a congregation of about ten, Celebrations on Saturdays, etc., but if we can get the huge attic licenced by the RE's to carry the weight of numbers, we shall move our Church up there. On Christmas Eve we had an early Celebration for a company of QWR's who were going up to the trenches for Christmas. In the evening we had a Festal Evensong, followed by a Celebration for night duty men; both were well attended, but there were no communicants that night — the natural feeling against making ones Communion at night is very strongly felt here; and those for whom I had intended it got off and came yesterday morning. Three chaps rigged up a glorious little Crib with lint, cotton wool, and a Christmas star. Then an electrician rigged up a tiny lamp off a dry battery to shine down from the top — they burnt it all down once after two day's work, trying to fix a candle — and it stood on a bamboo plant stand discovered in the garden, and draped beside the Carpenter's Bench altar. We had the Church furnished well with joyful guests at 7 and 8, and again at 11.30, both yesterday and today . . . Chap after chap said that they didn't think it possible to have spent so happy a Christmas away from home.

The chapel became very popular and, as news of it spread, it became apparent that its move to the large attic above was desirable.

Padre Harold Bates broke his leg on 19th December and for the two months of his absence Tubby worked for the most part on his own, even though being confined to bed himself on two occasions:

Tuesday, January 11th 1916 . . . I'm confined to the House at present by an episode which had both its ridiculous and painful side. About a week ago I had a party of QWR stretcher bearers — they are a glorious set of people, and had a very thin time of it with the gas attack on the 19th. Anyhow the French teapot refused to pour. No hatpins available so the leader of them, called Tiny — he is about as big as Neville Talbot — said "just blow down the spout, padre, it's the only way." I did so too heartily with the result that the lid came off and hot tea leaves all up my cheek. It was frightfully absurd at the time, but the burn has now cut up rusty and I have a bit of a swelling which the Labour Battalion MO has in hand; it is bandaged by the RAMC Corporal who is my chief of Staff (that's the best of these wonderful RAMC men), but for a day or so it means keeping inside Talbot House.

Six days later he was reporting another all too familiar illness:

I've got my old periodic go of malaria, that has come round so regularly three or four times a year. It's not the least serious and will probably get me a 48 hours holiday at Le Treport before the end of the week. Neville is coming himself to be OC Talbot House for a few days.

He was correct about his stay at Le Treport, but it took much longer than anticipated. With both Harold Bates and Tubby confined to bed, Neville Talbot brought in Dick Reid another 6th Division chaplain, together with Padre Crisford, 1st London Rifle Brigade to assist him in running the house.

Today, on one wall of this eight-roomed landing is an oak carving of Leonardo's *Last Supper*. Incomplete and rough hewn, except for the figure of the apostle, this work dates from the early to mid-eighteenth century. Originally the property of a Mr Flamand from Ypres who, mindful of his own safety, had moved to the south of France for the duration. It was bought from him for the sum of 75 francs. So concerned was Tubby about its safety that he had it packed in a valise and sent home to England where it spent the rest of the war.

Until 1995 the layout of the rooms on this landing was much different from that of today. A complete suite of rooms, known as "The Flat" or "Annex", was made up of one four-bedded and two single rooms adjoining plus a small kitchen area and a bathroom. Of today's eight rooms, six are named after personages connected with the house: Rolande Blanckaert, Angele Suffys, and her husband Sylvain Vandewalle, Barclay Baron, Arthur Lahaye, Jack Trefusis, Arthur Pettifer, and the other two, Archives Room and 5.9 (the bathroom) to commemorate the direct hit from a 5.9 inch shell.

**The Blanckaert Room** honours the memory of Rolande Blanckaert who ran a millinery shop a few yards away from the house. With a few friends Madame Blanckaert was the backbone of the Poperinghe "The Friends of The Old House" association which plays a very important part in all areas of the well being of the house, providing assistance with official and non-official functions held there.

**The Vandewalle Room** is named after Angele Suffys and her husband Sylvain Vandewalle who served as housekeepers during the period 1951 to 1971.

**The Barclay Baron Room**, named in memory of Tubby's close friend and constant visitor to the house. An assistant in the post war Toc H movement, his experiences during his time spent in Poperinghe during the war changed the direction of his life from that of a successful art historian and writer to a life working in Christian social service. It was dedicated to him on 21st September 1996, when his son David presented the Association with a floor tile his father had salvaged from Ypres Cathedral during the war.

**The Lahaye Room** commemorates Arthur Lahaye, the Burgomaster of Poperinghe during the Second World War. On one wall in the room there hangs a poem entitled *The Carpenter's Bench* by Reverend C. Cameron-Waller, Principal of Huron College, Canada.

**The Trefusis Room** was named on 20th September 1997, after Jack Trefusis, ex-Guards Officer, the first British officer to enter occupied Brussels after the Second World War D. Day landings. Noel Cornick, President of the Talbot House Association said of him:

> Toc H exhorts its members "to love widely, to build bravely, to think fairly and to witness humbly." Few can have followed these precepts with more devotion than Jack Trefusis.

On one wall in the room is the artwork for a pub sign, *The Old House At Home* showing an "Old Bill" type sitting in a wet, muddy trench dreaming of home. Presented to Talbot House in 1994 it carries the inscription *To The Old House, Poperinghe from Declan and Stephanie Burke, The Old House, Northampton*.

**The Archives Room** holds all that was in the old library together with artifacts, documents, paintings, photographs and items deemed too valuable to be on permanent display.

Albums of photographs taken by men during the war, when possessing a camera was forbidden, are kept here. Once on display, they were removed when a number of photographs were stolen. Paintings once hung in the Chapel but now needing restoration are also kept here, as does a 1913 Medici print, *The Holy Family*, given to Talbot House in 1930, inscribed *In memory of my husband Malcolmson G. Donahoe, MC. Capt. 8th Bn. KOYLI. Buried in Lijssenthoek Cemetery, Poperinghe*. Prized possessions are kept in the safe, amongst which is a replica of a Fairbairn-Sykes, Second World War commando dagger with a 22 carat gold handle and polished steel blade. Presented on behalf of Wilkinson Sword by Royal Mail, Northampton on 10th November 1994, one side of its blade carries the words *Manufactured by Royal swordsmiths, Wilkinson Sword, to commemorate the 50th anniversary of D. Day, 6th June 1944*, and Laurence Binyon's exhortation: *For The Fallen* on the other.

**The 5.9 Room** was named after the direct hit from a 5.9. shell during the summer of 1915. Repairs came within conditions of the tenancy agreement and a photograph of the rear of the house taken on 24th April 1916, shows the area boarded over. Word had it that the shell was a British "stray" but, whatever the case, the lack of damage caused would indicate that it was a dud.

**Pettifer's Den** named so after the quarters of a very special man to both Tubby and the people of Poperinghe. During the war years he was the only other permanent member of the staff; Tubby was extremely fond of him and went through a great deal of effort to keep him as his batman. Equally as fond of Tubby, Arthur Pettifer describes the effort made to keep him as a batman:

I was taken away, that was September 17th, 1917, from Tubby and sent to the Base to be reclassified, with a letter from 'im to 'and in, to have me sent back to 'im again. I 'anded the letter in to one of the sergeant-majors there, but whether the letter got 'anded in or not, I wasn't sent back to Tubby. So I was marked PB (permanent base) and put to a labour company in the Camerons, and got sent up to Dickebusch, an' I knew that if I could get down to Tubby I should be orl right.

So after a bit of trouble I managed to get a pass to go into Pop; and o' course made my way straight to Tubby. So 'e ses to me "Now I've got you I'm goin' to keep you." So I said to 'im, "You can't do that, I'm only on a few hours leave and I've got to go up the line working." (we were makin' a road called Warrington Road just off Hell Fire corner).

Tubby ses to me, "You come with me and we'll go and see a doctor." 'E took me to see a doctor in the "oo dee Fumes," an' 'e went in first and saw this doctor, and 'e ses I'm unfit to travel. An' next day they sent a despatch rider to Tubby to say "send Pte. Pettifer back" — Tubby sent a messenger back to say "the doctors orders are, he's unfit to travel" — and then my transfer from the 2nd Army to the 5th came through an' I was sent to the company; and the nex' message was "send Private Pettifer to bring his kit away!" An' I went up and got my kit, and the Captain 'ad gone on leave that mornin', or I dessay I'd 'ave got a tickin' orf. I guess 'e knew it was a wangle.

Tubby's own account in 1931 talks of Arthur Pettifer:

Permit me, therefore, to introduce you to the real old soldier — the "General" as he was universally known to three generations of clientele to Talbot House, Poperinghe, and to all the children of the neighbourhood who ran after him for shelter when the town was being shelled. On and off, by the year 1919, the Army had known him for thirty-one years as No. 239, Pte. Pettifer, A., 1st The Buffs, and although later attached on grounds of debility, to what was vulgarly known as an Area Enjoyment Company, the peak of his cap retained the dragon that no right-thinking man would desire to see replaced. He refused to put up his proper array of good conduct badges, as they would interfere with the set of his sleeve over his elbow. For chest protection he wore a Military Medal, an Indian frontier ribbon, the South African, and the so-called Mons. He is sagacious beyond belief in the ways and by-ways of the Army, which he entered as a band-boy in the year of my birth. A certain faded photograph of a cherub incredibly pipeclayed, and of a betrousered young warrior with an oiled forelock emerging beneath a hat like an inverted Panatella box, repose in his wallet, and may be seen by diplomatic approach on the subject of Brodrick caps. Long ago he might have put up sergeant's stripes; yea, and have been by now QMS, or even RSM; but he would not. Uneasy lies the arm that wears a crown, and to be the "General" is honour enough in his honest old eyes.

In the years between the South African War and the outbreak of the Great War, Pettifer lived in South Hackney, London, where he worked as a chauffeur:

... and drove a capacious cart. Trust an old infantryman to find something in peacetime to keep his feet off the ground.

Blessed with a good sense of humour, and an inoffensive nature, he believed everyone to be equally as honest as himself. He told of the time he took home a stranger who said that he was resuming to Australia but needed some money. Arthur lent him five shillings, against the better judgement of his wife. He never heard from the man again and, unable to fully accept that he could have been dishonest, with no intention of returning the five shillings, he said of the incident:

> I'm sure that young fellow sailed on one of them ships that was never heard of again! I give 'im my address and everything, but I never once 'ad a line from 'im from that day to this. 'An the missus didn't 'arf strafe neither!

With the outbreak of war he rejoined the Buffs, and:

> ... left the missus with one less dinner to see to, and the "nibs" without their Sunday escort.

In November 1914 his Regiment arrived in France, spending the winter in the Armentiéres sector, before moving into the Ypres Salient in May 1915. In the November of that year he was ordered to report to an unknown chaplain as batman.

> Pettifer, having at the first interview characteristically announced his inability to meet any domestic requirements, soon developed unique capacities in that direction. Shortly after we fetched up at Talbot House, his powers of acquisition made themselves felt. Like Horace in the "Brass Bottle", I became afraid to mention a need lest its fulfilment should bring disaster and disgrace. I was, for instance, overheard to say that a carpet for the Chapel was most desirable. Within an hour a carpet had arrived. Enquiry revealed the painful fact that it had come

from next door. "They won't be wanting it, sir; they do say the family are in the son' of France." It is incumbent upon the clergy to take their stand at such moments upon bedrock principles. "General, I can't say my prayers kneeling on a stolen carpet." Silence hereafter for a space: then a bright idea. "Well sir if yer won't 'ave it in the church, it'll do lovely for yer sitting room." When even this brilliant alternative is dismissed as Jesuitical, and the carpet restored to the place it came from, a few days elapse tranquilly. Then the "General" scores heavily one morning: "You remember that carpet sir?" I admit it. "Well, the ASC 'ave scrounged it now."

But God forbid that the "General" should be thought antisocial or unneighbourly. Nothing could be farther from the truth. This jackdaw trait is only in relation to things lying useless and idle, which none will miss; and it is more than out-weighed by a willingness to give of his own cheerfully whether or not it can easily be spared.

There was, moreover, not a child in Poperinghe whose face did not light up at his approach. It was they who conferred upon him the title of "le General", by which he was greeted in every narrow street. And to many of the old folk as well he has been a benefactor in dark days; wheeling their "sticks" away to safety, or greatly concerned for the still more difficult removal of the bed-ridden.

Fancy, bed-ridden old people, in a town shelled such as Poperinghe has been.

It was part of Arthur's duties to attend to Tubby when he was sick and Captain Leonard Browne, Royal Army Medical Corps speaks of an experience with Arthur:

To make quite sure no one could disturb him when his temperature was about 105, I put the old "General" on duty at his door to keep out anyone who might ignore the notice. On returning in the evening I was touched to find the "General" "asleep at his post" in a chair. He had probably been up all the night before, but he awakened up covered with confusion, rather feeling that he had let down the tradition of The Buffs. However, when I came back the same time next evening I was seized by the arm in the dim light, while a hoarse voice whispered: "You can't go in, sir; it's the Doctor's orders." It was flattering to feel that my instructions were so faithfully carried out after the lapse of the previous day.

Pettifer's reply to a letter from Tubby in a Boulogne hospital reads:

MY DEAR SIR
Don't be alarmed, the old General is still alive and kicking. I think it is almost time I answered your letter, don't you? Never mind, you are a long way from me and cannot hit me — Ah, ah! Well myself

and young Vok are very pleased you are coming back again. Of course you know there has been a great change in both houses. Sergt. Godley and his men have left us, also Mr. Talbot, and Mr. Talbot told me he had a very hard struggle with my Colonel to keep me. Fancy you coming back to find me in the trenches, once more popping at the boshes! Old Fritz has not sent us any iron rations over for four weeks now, he generally pays a visit about every six weeks, so I suppose we can look out for him. I feel sorry you are so lonely there. Never mind it's a long way to Tipperary, I mean a long lane that has no turning. Sergt. Godley and the lads all wished to be remembered to you before they went. Myself and young Vok send our love to you and don't forget when you come back — to bed early. We'll see that you don't get knocked up again in a hurry. Well close now with love from the old GENERAL.

Tubby once remarked that, as a servant, Arthur Pettifer played Sancho Panza to his Don Quixote. He habitually called Tubby "Sir", even after the war, and strongly disapproved of the pseudonym "Tubby".

So much for the eight rooms on this floor, a floor that, in 1916, served as an "Ante Chapel" or "Chamber". To the immediate left of the stairway leading to it is a part-glazed door which, when opened, gives access to a very steep stairway called Jacob's Ladder. Thousands of army-booted feet in the past trod this ladder to reach the famous Talbot House Chapel — the Upper Room.

**107**

# CHAPER
# SEVEN

# The Upper Room

Here is a quiet room!
Pause for a little space;
And in the deepening gloom,
With hands before thy face,
Pray for God's Grace.

*Donald Cox*

The Chapel or Upper Room, today is complete in almost every detail to what it was in the war years. It was at the insistence of Padre Crisford that the Chapel was moved here in late January 1916, with 500 men of the London Rifle Brigade and 200 of the Queen's Westminster Rifles taking communion over the Christmas period bringing strong influence to bear on the decision. From 25th to 31st January, structural tests were carried out by the Royal Engineers to determine the load-bearing capabilities of the floor:

There ensued a series of consultations which grew gloomier in ascending ratio of rank. First two London sappers danced on it, and assured us cheerily that it would stand anything. So far so good. But the lance-corporal in charge of them shook his head with the pregnant pessimism of Lord Burleigh himself. An appeal was lodged with the sergeant over him, who expressed the gravest doubts. Next the lieutenant immediately concerned tapped and condemned the joists. His captain came in one day and verbally countersigned this adverse verdict. The major of the Field Company trod as delicately as Agag, and left us a prey to an hourly expectation of spontaneous collapse. In despair, we appealed to Colonel Tannett-Walker, who, after personal inspection, had the details of the floor worked out and presented in triplicate, proving conclusively that the attic was wholly unsafe. After this we asked no more questions, but opened the Chapel therein without more ado.

On his return from Boulogne on 1st February Tubby wrote:

We have moved the Chapel into the attic, which makes a perfectly beautiful Church, with hangings from the Bishop's Chapel at Southwark. We have a Daily Celebration at 7.15 which means I am getting to bed earlier and a faithful few are beginning to come in regularly. Evensong at 7.15 at night is well attended.

The transformation of the "old" chapel to the "new" was handled by men of the Queen's Westminster Rifles. Using pictures of the scriptures from old books as reference, men of the Motor Machine-Gun Company painted the windows, giving them the appearance of stained glass. The carpenters bench was placed on a dais under a wooden framework which was then transformed into a baldachino from drapes provided by the Bishop of Winchester. An altar frontal, presented by Lieutenant Stokes in memory of the officers and men of the Guards Division, was handcrafted by the Wantage Sisters of Holy Cross Court, Haywards Heath. A number of altar accoutrements were to follow: a silver gilt communion chalice with a fine lace veil made by local nuns, was given by 6th Field Ambulance; flower vases atop the altar, the gift of Lady Byng of Vimy and, above the altar, a Medici print of Perugino's *Crucifixion Triptych* framed in the gold-painted top of an old bamboo table by Lance-Corporal Bert Stagg of The Queen's Westminster Rifles. Hanging from the central roof beam is a crucifix made by 120th Railway Construction Company. Its figure of Christ being found, muddy and rusty on the canal bank at "Dead End", Ypres. A portable harmonium, later nicknamed "The Groan Box", given to the house by Major Edmond Street D.S.O. of the Sherwood Foresters, completed the main furnishings of the chapel.

After the war soldier graves were marked by The Graves Registration Unit with simple wooden crosses, replaced in the 1920's and '30's, with headstones. A number of the original markers from the graves of unknown soldiers are to be found in the Chapel. That of Gilbert Talbot, to the left of the altar, is his second grave marker. The original, in the form of a Celtic Cross, placed on the grave by his brother Neville in the company of Canon Scott, Chaplain to the Canadian forces, was kept in the Coeur de Lion Chapel, All Hallows, London until 1940. This second marker was found one morning propped against the front door of the house. Someone had put it there, rang the doorbell and left, having kept it for over forty years.

The altar is approached by a broad Sanctuary. Erring on the side of caution with the weakness of the floor in mind, it was decided that the congregation should be seated at the sides rather than in rows from front to rear. This put the Sanctuary at the heart of the congregation.

A visitor wrote:

It was 1917, and a warm Sunday in July. We were at Poperinghe, about 5 miles behind the lines, and I and my friends had spent the day at Talbot House, known more familiarly by the signalese rendering of its initials, Toc H. Now more than ninety of us had crowded into the Upper Room, with another twenty sitting or standing on the stairs, the backs of the seated twisted uncomfortably in a gesture of polite attention to the chaplain, Philip Clayton. As the final hymn was announced, we moved together, faltered guiltily, and then scrambled to our feet in an untidy and unmilitary fashion. The floorboards of the attic were known to be unsafe, and we had been asked to stagger our movements — an instruction repeated several times at each service, but still difficult for trained soldiers to remember. It was not only the floorboards that were rickety.

The harmonium was weak at the knees; and it had real knees, having been designed to fold up and fit into the side car of Tubby Clayton's motor cycle when he visited the field hospitals and casualty clearing stations. But there was nothing wrong with its sound, and a hush fell as the organist produced a grand chord from the unlikely instrument. Voices were raised, and the Old Hundredth boomed out, its pace accelerated perhaps by an attempt to disguise the Germanic origins of the tune from those few who might be aware of them, or simply by the organist's energetic pumping of the pedals. Was it an appropriate hymn to have chosen, I wondered, for men who would go into battle before the week was out? Could we really praise God at this time? Tubby had preached that evening on the need to praise Him at all times, and for real believers, this was the logical position. I was no longer a real believer, but this was no time to reopen an old debate. And German or not, the stirring tune and the voices in unison fostered a sense of companionship not to be spurned. I joined wholeheartedly in the singing and felt better about the coming week.

Tubby spoke of the danger of the floor collapsing:

Times were when it repented us of our rashness, but we lived to repent of our repentance. On Sunday nights, for years on end, with a hundred and fifty grown men squeezed in somehow, and twenty more upon the stairs, the Chapel rocked like a huge cradle, until we were fain to ask a congregation drilled into habits of simultaneous movement to kneel and stand in lingering succession. On occasions of shelling or bombing, or (once) of both these amenities together, the Chapel might readily have carried the congregation with it. One Sunday night in July 1917, there were nearly a hundred casualties at Poperinghe Station during Evensong in the Chapel. March 18th 1918, a Quiet Day conducted by the Bishop of Lewes was held in spite of a slow methodical shelling. Several "obus" landed within fifty yards of the Chapel, but the Quiet day went on. I can recall Celebrations and Confessions with similar accompaniments.

The Germans had installed a railway-mounted, long-range gun ten miles away. At infrequent intervals, day and night, it would open fire with five or six rounds in quick succession. One morning Tubby climbed to the Chapel for early Communion and finding a number of men there he began performing the service. Having given the blessing:

I turned back again to the low altar, when suddenly, so swift and sharp that it was heralded by no fierce scream of warning, the great gun opened. The first shell skimmed the high roof above our heads, and plunged with a roar into the private field behind the garden ... The picture in my mind was this; the floor would go first, with it the benches and the

113

altar; chalice and paten would be spilled, and all in one great heap lie tangled, smoking disannulled, as one had often seen in the houses thus demolished. Shells had been close before, but never quite so heavy; and in another moment the next would come ... The next shell came. Its line of flight was almost as before, but those fine gunners had learned the first had fallen short of the switch-road, and given that tiny access of elevation which bracketed their target. More rounds followed while our service ended.

In excess of 25,000 men took Communion in the chapel with many being served from the chapel's silver vessels. In 1916 a silver wafer box was donated in memory of Rifleman Newton Gammon, Queen's Westminster Rifles, who died on the Somme, and the same year a Miss Becket and the poor of Beeston St. Portsea gave the house a four and a half inch high Pyx, a portable Communion vessel. The top half, made of silver in the shape of a gabled roof top with dormer windows, served to transport the consecrated bread for services in the field and when ministering to the sick. The bottom half, made of glass, carried the wine. The silver topped rim is inscribed: *A Pyx for the great Gift of Love, from the poor of Beeston Street, Portsmouth, to the B.E.F* Tubby carried this Pyx with him whenever he conducted a service in the field.

In 1930 a silver chalice and paten were given in memory of Clifford Reed, M.C., who fell at Messines, the first Wesleyan chaplain to be killed in the war.

At the turn of the century the Church served not only as a place of worship, but somewhere to learn and meet friends. Bible and confirmation classes were commonplace and Talbot House offered the same facilities to its parish. Holy Communion services were a daily feature in the chapel. At Easter 1916:

That first Holy Week. The daily services were full, and the Three Hours Service conducted by Neville drew together a cluster of about fifty Christian men (among them the Corps Commander), seated between a lieutenant and a private, intent upon a common homage. Only the day before there had been bloody doings near the canal at Boesinghe, when a company of the Bedfords had been blown by a whirlwind concentration out of a miserable travesty of a trench — E35, I think, and the tale of the Agony and the Darkness fell upon our ears with a new sense of kinship. Easter Eve brought us gifts of spring flowers not only gathered in the ruined gardens of Ypres and Goldfisch (Rozelaar) Chateau by our own men, but also great bunches of bloom from some Belgian nuns hard by ... the Chapel was transformed into the most perfect place of worship in Belgium. Easter Day, 1916, I shall always regard as the happiest of my ministry. We had no past evidence to assist in estimating the number of Communicants to be expected. It was quite possible, especially in view of the lively state of the line, that only a few would be able to attend. The event far surpassed our hopes. We had about

270 Communicants, the Divisional General, most of the Staff, Brigadiers, Colonels, Bandsmen, Signallers, Railway men, RAMC, ASC, MT, RE's, Infantry, Motor Machine Gunners, Heavy Gunners, Armourers, Army Ordnance Men, Red Cross folk, and even a sergeant of the AVC. If the Chapel floor had collapsed at 8, 9.30 or 11.30 (as it ought to have done by all laws of gravity) practically every branch of the Army here would have had its representative in the common ruin! Not only was every Celebration furnished with joyful guests but so great was the throng, and so divergent their estimates of time, that the whole of the floor below the Chapel was full of congregations waiting to replace that already above. Single handed as I was, I could do no more than Lift and Break and give without pause from 5.30 until after noonday, those that were fed being above four hundred men . . . The 11.30 service I shall always remember, as indeed I think will all those who were there — about a hundred, half of whom had returned to give thanks for their Communion earlier. We sang Merbecke and Easter hymns all through . . . greatly aided by Godfrey Gardiner in the further loft, and by some of the Welsh Guards' choir. The congregation had long ago overflowed its benches and men knelt where they could.

Douglas Legg in writing of that service said:

. . . we crowded into the Upper Room to greet the risen Christ. Many more were waiting before the altar. When I think back to that Easter Day I have often wondered at the supernatural strength that must have been given to Tubby on that occasion, for he showed no sign of fatigue.

Lance-Corporal Harry Moss, of the Essex Regiment comments:

Easter Day, 1916, 7a.m., and the Upper Room is full; officers and men, the little Padre officiating; been there since 5.30a.m. — so I'm told after. No more room, have to wait on that shaky old ladder. Goodness, what a crowd! Generals too, all sorts and conditions. He has to make the service short; just break and lift and give without pause, all these hours — over 400 men being fed. Some are descending the ladder that leads to the Upper Room, only one at a time can manage it. I wonder how many of them will come back again, poor devils, got to keep going up into that hell of Ypres.

Nurses from the nearby Field Ambulance units and hospitals often visited and, at Easter 1917, Alison Macfie from the Belgian Red Cross hospital at La Panne wrote:

We were tremendously thrilled to be for a time among the British units, and close to the heroic defenders of the Salient of Ypres. The Easter

Festival came while we were at Couthove, and we asked if we could possibly attend an English service. We were therefore taken by ambulance to Poperinghe on Easter morning and there deposited outside the big iron-work doors of Talbot House in the Rue de l'Hopital. I have a hazy recollection of many people about the place, as we were conducted up the stairs to the upper floors. I do remember very distinctly, on climbing up the steep stair to the Upper Room, reaching the level of the floor with my head, I looked around and saw nothing but a sea of very muddy boots and khaki puttees, all much the same in colour. There had been a service going on continuously since dawn, and still the Chapel was crowded. Room was made for us, and we knelt before that sacred Bench beside men for whom this was a rare and deeply valued opportunity in the dark and dangerous life of the trenches around Ypres . . . When we came down from the Upper Room we found the Padre who had taken the service greeting the congregation as it stood about in the hall or vanished into the garden or out into the street.

From Tubby's own journals:

27th April 1917. The Chapel looked perfectly divine, flowers everywhere, from Settle and elsewhere, a new altar cloth, worked (unknown by me) by the sister of an RE friend of more than a years standing. I scrounged an organist from a neighbouring Territorial Band, so that we had hymns 134, 136 and 140 in continual succession. More and more officers and men flocked in, so that the landing and stairs below the Upper Room were crowded with their waiting until the Service before was completed.

Private services were also part of the house function. In early 1916, a Canadian sergeant about to go on leave and, too early for his train's departure, decided to visit the house. He said that his parents were missionaries in Japan and that he would like to visit the chapel. The sergeant, with Tubby, sat and prayed there. Later in the day, shortly before his train was due, an orderly from his battalion arrived with a message to say his leave had been postponed as he was to give evidence at a court-martial the following day. Once again he and Tubby climbed to the Chapel and this time prayed for his safety and the hope that his return to duty would not defer his leave for too long. The sergeant left with the promise to return when his papers were re-issued.

For weeks after I awaited his return; until I found that his battalion had been hard pressed in a sudden emergency and that he himself had been killed.

On Monday, 10th April 1916, Tubby wrote of another instance:

. . . this afternoon an utter stranger, an officer, came in and asked shyly if he might go up to the Chapel

**119**

and be quiet. I, in response, asked if I could be of any help if I went up to him there. He accepted gladly, and after a little time I followed him. It turned out he had just had news of his father's death at home. The news had been delayed in reaching him owing to his regiment moving, and the funeral was to be at 3 this afternoon. So at 3 in the Chapel I held the Burial Service with a quiet congregation of one: and he went back to his regiment I think with his sorrow somewhat assuaged.

He often said there were three in attendance at these services held at one of the two prayer desks, one dedicated to Kenneth Mayhew, 6th London Regiment, and William Wellings Locke, 133 Field Ambulance, and the other to Lieutenant Bernard Stenning, who died in July 1917.

Australian Tunnellers fashioned two altar candlesticks from corner posts of a four-poster bed *in memorium* to their officers who had taken Communion in the chapel. A Lieutenant of a Kent regiment who had taken Communion at the same time offered to design them, but:

... his great friend came to me much moved with the news that he had been killed the night before, dying very nobly. A patrol from his battalion had been out and on its return spotted; he had gone out to bring in a wounded sergeant, and had done so successfully, but on going out again for another wounded man, himself was killed.

A third candlestick dedicated to Lieutenant G. Willan Morris, King's Own Yorkshire Light Infantry, was donated by his brother officers and serves as a stand for the "Winton Font", a six inches square white biscuit-china replica of the black marble font in Winchester Cathedral. It belonged to Tubby's mother and in 1885, it was used to baptise him. She sent it to him and, in September 1915, he first used it to baptise a dying man:

I can well remember the scene . . . with a drummer boy kneeling by the side of Sergt. Berry's stretcher at the entrance to a hospital tent.

It was used frequently for baptism, the last time at Evensong in November 1917, for four British West Indian ammunition carriers.

At the actual moment of baptism five Chinamen, who had somehow made their way into the House and up to the top of it, climbed the steep staircase to the Chapel and stood quietly witnessing the Ceremony, the significance of which it is possible they grasped in some measure without interpretation.

There were seldom less than a hundred in attendance at Holy Communion and those who took it completed a simple form, part of Tubby's "Communicants Roll", a register kept with the intention to contact all those listed after the war. The Church had foreseen the need for more clergymen after the war and Tubby kept another list of ordination candidates, men who wished to join the clergy "when it was all over". During the war around 800 men were confirmed in the chapel, nearly 50 were baptised, and over 25,000 took Communion.

The "Archbishop's" or "Confirmation Chair" in the chapel converts to a round-topped table. It bears a plate inscribed *To the Glory of God and the Memory of Archie Forrest, "P" Coy. Spl. Gas. Baptised and Confirmed in this Chapel, Killed in Action 1917. From the Friends of Archie Forrest.*

Archie Forrest first visited the house in June 1917 with Sergeant George Dewdney, a regular church-goer. Archie was of little conviction, but found the fellowship to his liking and, even though working every night in the Salient, managed to visit almost daily. Soon after his first visit to the chapel he asked to be baptised. As Tubby puts it:

> ... this tall, lean, quick and curly haired, Lancashire lance corporal with an element of fierceness in doing what he did with all his might found in Talbot House the true birthplace of his soul.

He attended his first class on 9th July and was confirmed six weeks later. He was later killed and now lies buried in Wieltje Farm Cemetery.

The oak figure of a kneeling monk holding a chalice is inscribed: *This carving was found in the ruins of Velu (Somme) in 1916 and was brought to Talbot House by Smith-Gunner Charles Payne, 18th Siege Battery, whose body lies at Brielen.*

A small gilt-framed copy of the painting "Venez a Moi", is inscribed *In loving memory of Edmund Street, D.S.O., Major, 2nd Sherwoods. Killed September 1916 on the Somme.* After being notified of his death his sister sent ten guineas to the house. The painting was bought for ten shillings and the remaining ten pounds were used to found the Ordination Candidates Fund. To the right of the altar hangs the first "In Memoriam Roll" of the house. Amongst the 46 listed, it begins with Gilbert Talbot"s name, is poet John McCrae author of "In Flanders Fields". Another is that of Captain Noel G. Chavasse, MC., VC and Bar, who would always visit when in the vicinity of the house. The roll was later published as a book entitled *Liber Vitae of Toc H.* a copy of which is on display in All Hallows Church, London.

Of the chapel contents Tubby was to write:

This inventory of ornaments is, perhaps, a tale of little worth in the judgement of those who are accustomed to the lavish elegancies of a home parish. Yet such will bear with me, when they remember how far a little beauty went amid such surroundings as ours. To live day by day not only in danger but in squalor; to be gypsies in season and out, in a nightmare fit for Cain; to be homeless amid all that is hideous and disheartening, habituated to a foreground of filth and a horizon of apparently invincible menace; to move always among the wreckage of mens lives and hopes, haunted not only by a sense of being yourself doomed to die, but by an agony of mind which cried out at every step against the futile folly of the waste of time and of treasure, of skill and of life itself — this is what war meant to a soul sensitive to such impressions . . . Thus it was that the homely beauty of the Chapel, with its inward gift of hope and fellowship, drew many who learnt their hunger in the grimmest school which the spirit of man has yet experienced; and eyes hardened by indomitable will to withstand the brutalising obscenities of war, softened to appraise our simple seeking after sweetness and light.

In 1916, Lance-Corporal Lowman, M.M., Queen's Westminster Rifles completed a drawing of the altar of which E. W. Charlton, R.E. made an etching. It was published as Tubby puts it:

. . . without acknowledgement, in illustrated papers, under such absurd titles as "a Chapel in the front line trenches"

Other renderings were produced during the war by Kenneth Barfield, Cecil Worsley and Barclay Baron. In 1921, the Imperial War Museum commissioned Herbert H. Cawood to construct a model of the chapel. Three were made, one is on permanent display in the museum, another is in All Hallows Church, London and the third in the "In Flanders Fields" museum, Ypres.

# CHAPTER
# EIGHT

# In The Field

The cherry trees bend over and are shedding,
On the old road where all that passed are dead,
Their petals, strewing the grass as for a wedding
This early May morn when there is none to wed.
                                        *Edward Thomas*

The house parish embraced any local field unit wanting
a padre's services, in particular The Buffs (East Kent
Regiment) and Bedfordshire Regiment of 16th Infantry
Brigade. In his early days with the 6th Division Tubby
saw his work as being:

> ... of the bush brotherhood type ... services for all
> kinds of scattered units, entailing a journey per
> man of some fifty miles a week, riding, walking
> and wading; but a real rough welcome and some
> kind of pot-luck wherever one goes. Then there are
> the rather ghastly funerals in places more or less
> accessible, and the caring for the men who are
> "resting" after so many days and nights in the
> advance trenches. Our work naturally entails a

good deal of roughing it, mud, wet, cold and weariness.

Rarely a day passed when he did not go "slumming", as he called it:

It had become my custom to spend one day and night each week with the three Batteries which were my forward flock. Pettifer and I for three years thus set out together, generally on Thursday morning, returning to Talbot House on Friday. All sorts of units in turn lent transport to ferry our spiritual munitions to and fro. These included a baby Pathe Cinema and one or two tins of films, one sandbag holding hymn-books and Communion Services, another full of printed matter, my Communion case (always called the Crown Jewels case), the State Paper case, Edmund Street's portable harmonium, and several other human frailties, including several tins of Mrs Fry's Cocoa. From all this stuff we were easily separable. Sometimes it went by luggage in advance, and lay waiting our arrival at No. 10 bridge Ypres, where the first tin of cocoa might be broached. It travelled by every method, and at every speed, from the general supply wagon or the gun limber, to the breathless luxury of Godfrey Pope's box car, or a Flying Corps tender. If we had calls to make on the way up, we might travel with it to Vlamertinghe and then kiss it goodbye until tomorrow or some other day. The astounding thing was, not that it disappeared, but that it all came home . . .

Monday, December 22nd 1916 . . . I'll just jot down my week's programme, for your amusement and reference. It's much the same each week:

Sunday. Celebrations at 6.30, 7.30a.m. Service with Artillery workshops at 9.15a.m. Morning service at TH (chiefly Signal school) 10.30. Eucharist with hymns 11.30. Bible Class 3p.m. CEMS social meeting 4.45p.m. Men's Prayer meeting 5.15p.m. Evensong 6.30p.m.

Monday. Celebration 7.30a.m. (2 each week-day). 2p.m. Police Service. If I get up early enough, I visit a battery section before-hand, and lunch with them or Winterbotham. Return to TH for tea with various men. Evensong 6p.m. 6.30p.m. Lecture (lantern) by SCF of a neighbouring division on China tonight.

Tuesday. At home during the day till after Evensong. 5.30p.m. Whist-drive in TH. Go up to Anti-Aircraft service at 7.00p.m. and stop to dinner, returning at 10p.m.

Wednesday. At home all day, plus visiting of local units. After Evensong, a men's debate on Industrial Conscription — i.e. munition workers in khaki at soldiers pay. Last week in crowded House (i.e.

about 200) the motion carried that "the war would be over by August."

Thursday. I leave TH early in afternoon, B'ty section (Advanced) service at 5p.m. Another at B'ty HQ after a miles walk between them, at 7p.m. Dinner and sleep there.

Friday. Celebration at B'ty HQ at 8a.m. Breakfast afterwards. Service with some Field Survey folk at 11a.m. Lunch with them or elsewhere. Service with bobbies in — at 3p.m. Catch a lift home. Service at TH 6p.m. Shakespeare reading (a group of about 15 keen folk) at 6.30p.m.

Saturday. At home mostly. CEMS discussion of Ordination proposals 6.30.

Well organised as this may seem, Captain Leonard Browne noted:

Only one who had no idea of time or space or money could possibly have carried on at Talbot House. PBC regarded time as an arbitrary division of the day; space was better ignored. One of his favourite dicta, on which he acted with great fidelity, was "the only way to arrive in time is to start out late: if you start punctually you will probably never arrive". Occasionally he proved this by experience.

In the late summer of 1916 Tubby was unofficially attached to 141 (East Ham) Heavy Battery, Royal Garrison Artillery, at Vlamertinghe. Commanding Officer, Colonel L. H. Higgon, asked that Tubby perform a service for his men at 2.30p.m. on a Sunday. On the day, a large congregation had gathered and waited until 3.25 when Tubby arrived, sweating profusely, laden with gas-mask, sandbags of hymn-books and other items, stumbling through the long grass, with Pettifer, carrying the portable harmonium and more bags of books, struggling along behind him. Toward the end of the service a dog positioned itself opposite Tubby and barked every time he opened his mouth to speak. This continued until Tubby turned to the dog and said in a loud voice:

> If you will be good enough to let me finish what I have to say, your turn will follow.

And the dog stopped barking. Colonel Higgon, who was to become a lifelong friend of Tubby's, said of the service:

> ... most of us felt that there was something about this service one too often misses in the ordinary church parade — an indefinable homeliness, a sort of genuine friendliness.

On another visit, Higgon found Tubby at breakfast with a Lieutenant Hopkinson. Asking if Tubby was "doing alright," he was told:

I assure you, I am not doing badly for a high-church curate on the first Friday in Lent.

He frequently risked travelling through "no-go" areas to visit his parish and "running for cover" became one of his pastimes when in the field. Services were regularly held with the congregation, Tubby, harmonium and organist, all huddled together in a shell-hole. Another of his favourite pastimes was scrounging lifts from army transports, staff drivers, motor machine-gun cyclists,; the Railway Operating Department and any other vehicle which was moving in the direction he wanted to take. One night while looking for a lift, he mistakenly took a locomotive to be one that was driven by a friend. He knocked on the driver's door and, on receiving no reply, threw a rock at it. The driver, who turned out not to be his friend, opened the door and hit him on the head with a shovel. Fortunately, he was wearing his steel helmet.

He was often exposed to danger when making his field visits, as on Easter Sunday 1916:

At 12.30 Colonel Hutchinson carried Gardiner, myself, and the little harmonium off to lunch at his group headquarters on the Elverdinghe Road. After an Easter service there, we went on to one of his batteries at Fantasio Farm. The afternoon was spring-like, and a Boche aeroplane was directing some target practice on Hale's Farm a few hundred yards away, which was used as a storehouse for hand-grenades. The farm was alight, its contents detonating in a staccato manner. Our car swung round the narrow corner beyond the brewery at Elverdinghe, and awakened the malicious interest of the observer, who bracketed on the road behind and in front of us. By this time we were almost alongside Fantasio Farm, and the adjutant ordered us to tumble out with the harmonium, and make our way to our destination while he piloted the car out of danger. This we did, and, after a short respite in a friendly ditch, proceeded towards the ruin previously pointed out to us, carrying the harmonium, hymn-books, and Communion case. The farm looked deserted in the extreme, but we were not a little cheered by a notice-board on an adjacent tree trunk displaying the following:

*Fantasio Farm. "B.21.d.5.9."*
*Lost travellers cared for. Lonely soldiers*
*corresponded with. Teas for tourists at short notice.*
*You may telephone from here.*

That evening he was summoned to No. 17 Casualty Clearing Station to visit Aubrey Colwell, an ex-orderly of the house who had been wounded. On arriving in the vicinity of the clearing station, he instructed his driver to stop whilst he set out on foot across the fields to find it. Reaching a railway track he followed it until he came to a bridge, with two stationary trains barring his way across it. He managed to reach Aubrey Colwell at the clearing station by crawling along the rails beneath the trains, commenting on his return at the end of the day:

When I returned to Talbot House I was more than grateful for my Sunday supper of soup and tinned sausages.

Shortly afterwards he wrote to Colwell's sister:

Easter Monday. Dear Miss Colwell, Yesterday evening I heard the bad news that your dear brother had been wounded; so I got hold of a machine gun motor and went to see him in the Casualty Clearing Hospital. I found him much better than I had dared to hope, and then the Doctor, who is a great friend of mine, gave me an excellent report of him. The wound is severe, but not dangerous; thank God. It is close to the shoulder, and he also has a rib broken. He will probably be at the CCS for 3 or 4 days, and then sent down the line: I expect he will be in England in a week or so.

And to his fiancée:

Easter Tuesday. Dear Miss Davis, You will have heard by now of Aubrey being wounded. I saw him again yesterday at the Casualty Clearing Hospital, and he asked me to write to you. He is doing wonderfully well, thank God, and will be down the line in a few days, and in England not long afterwards I expect. The wound in his chest is serious, but not dangerous; and not very painful now. He chats away cheerily and has no anxiety except that you and his family will be so distressed.

The Doctor tells me he should make a complete recovery, though it will mean some time at home. He's certainly done his bit out here. He's a really good fellow and means a lot to me. Yours in sincere sympathy, (Rev.) P.B. Clayton.

On another field trip to Railway Dugouts, for a service with the 154 (Southampton Territorial) Heavy Battery, Tubby and Pettifer took lunch with the subalterns before the service. No sooner had they finished eating when the enemy opened a heavy bombardment on the position and they and the congregation quickly took cover in a dugout:

> ... and as some shells were by their sound gas shells we dropped the gas curtain behind us.

Tubby passed around his hymn sheets and, with the subaltern, sat in the dugout entrance, starting the service with the hymn "Hold the Fort". When the service ended, Tubby pulled back the gas curtain to find the body of a dead signaller, the Major's orderly, who had only been married six months and Tubby had witnessed his Confirmation in Talbot House two weeks previously. He and the subaltern moved the body so that the men leaving the dug-out would not see it.

On noticing that four signallers were missing, he enquired as to their whereabouts and was told they were on duty in a position fifty yards away:

I made my way towards them, and found them crouching on the slope of the embankment where the shelling was still heavy, though intermittent. As they could not leave their instruments, the only way was to minister to them in the open. And there, upon the side of the embankment, we five men knelt down together. After a few words of the prayers, I opened the upper part of the Pyx to minister therefrom. Having done so, I felt for the tiny lock whereby the lower portion of the Pyx (this part of glass) might be freed for the second ministration.

At this moment the air immediately above our heads was filled with the bursting of a shell. We had all taken off our tin hats, and knelt there entirely unprotected. The shell burst perhaps fifteen feet up, and every bush about us was cut with flying fragments. The whole air was charged, as it seemed, with that unmistakable sound of metal whining and thudding to the ground. Not one of us was touched: I would almost say not one of us was frightened. Completely deaf for the moment, I ministered from the Cup, replaced its cover, said the Lord's Prayer, and rose from one knee to give the Peace.

A few moments later I left them and stumbled down the slope to summon Pettifer and pass upon our way. We did this without, so far as I remember, any further incident. But what further could there be to equal those which I had witnessed in that last half-hour? Mine eyes had indeed seen His salvation.

A fatalist, on 17th January 1916, Tubby wrote:

. . . one gets so used to the idea of death that one comes to realise, as Edmund Street, a brave man, said to me yesterday, death is far from being the worst thing that can happen to a man.

It was this philosophy that prompted him to further write:

I'm afraid Lewin has been killed. I'm rather coming to the conclusion that death must be a tremendous reward in cases such as this, so dazzling a joy that it has to be wrapped up in an ugly parcel or it would blind us. If this is really so, how we shall smile beyond to think of the fuss we made about it here.

He went on most field trips with Pettifer and the harmonium. Nicknamed "The Old Groan Box" it had been machine gunned, blown-up and often left at battery positions whilst he went elsewhere, being retrieved on his return journey. Long after the war he received a note from a Roman Catholic padre serving in occupied Germany:

Box 342, Army Post Office S/40, Wiesbaden, 16-8-27. My Dear Sir, Before the Army was moved from Cologne, I was given by the RC Chaplain, a "useless" old organ (by Southsea and Siebert, Petersfield). After much cleaning of the reeds and case I have made use of it. But what might interest you is this: On carefully cleaning a label inside the cover I made out the following indistinct writing: The Chants . . . Dim . . . one to be found on the 10th . . . and 23rd evenings . . . and the Congregation to sing . . . original key. No other chants . . . Evensong.
27.3. 1(6)?. By Order of the Chaplain. P.B.C.

On lately discovering the initials "PBC" and the doubtful last figure "6", I had what is very possibly the wild idea that this harmonium might have been used at Toc H. At any rate if the instrument has any associations with, or has any value to you, it shall travel back to its original possessor. It most obviously has never been RC property. I am leaving the Rhine Army in September, and will bring it back to England if you desire. J. St. Clair Goldie, CF.

A copy of the above is today attached to the harmonium with a footnote added by Tubby:

And, behold! the old organ, used in 1917 in the Concert Hall in the garden of Talbot House, Poperinghe, when congregations were too big for

137

the Upper Room, returns to claim its Old Age Pension.

Written in 1932:

... this veteran groan-box now reposes voiceless in the Chapel of the Old House

That year a Mr Ernest P. Daynes finished his apprenticeship as a piano tuner/repairer. In 1980 he visited the house, asked after the harmonium, and was told that it was unusable. In 1981 it was taken to England and he and a colleague, Arthur Kitch, repaired and refurbished it. Returned to the house, it was put out of order again by the constant attempts by heavy-handed visitors to play it, and now rests, voiceless once more, in the chapel.

# CHAPTER
# NINE

# 1918

"This house," said the old Bishop to Jean Valjean,
"is not my house but God's; and is open
not to him that hath a name but to him that hath a need."
*Victor Hugo.*

As Third Ypres drew to a close in November 1917, Tubby noted a sense of despondency and a lowering of morale amongst both officers and men:

> An evil spirit for the first time troubled both officers and men; and in the inevitable stagnation the phantom of failure, ridiculed before, walked grimly abroad and was not always challenged.

Determined that Christmas 1917 would be celebrated in the traditional way, Tubby sent out 2,000 Christmas cards based on his Communicants Roll, and feted the local children. Sharing his thoughts to his mother:

> I'm afraid the next few months are going to be very hard on the boys, the Boche very strong and fierce, thanks to Russian impotence; but we shall weather

the storm with God's help. And I feel more convinced as the time goes on that we must go on too. I should not relish the task of going to the women in black at home and saying, "It was all a mistake. There was no need for him to have died at all."

In an attempt to bolster morale and counteract these negative feelings, "grousing circles" were introduced in the house. These meetings were attended by a number of Garrison Staff officers who took notes, aired opinions, and offered advice. Under King's regulations these meetings had no place but, after a number had been held and problems were successfully resolved, their worth was realised, officially sanctioned and encouraged. Although nothing could be done to improve the conditions the men were forced to endure in the line:

The chief causes of complaint were simple in the extreme — the admitted injustice of the distribution of leave, the inequitable distribution of the bread and biscuit ration, in which the infantry (as usual) came out the losers, the absence of restaurant accommodation for men, the grotesque inequalities of pay, and so forth.

Many of the problems raised were perhaps petty but felt to warrant a fair hearing. By this means those attending the grousing circles could be assured of an equal and unbiased hearing, whilst those with the power to do so attempted to find solutions.

On 13th November 1917, Tubby had opened Little Talbot House in what was once L' Ecole de Dentelle in Rue de Lille, Ypres. Under the leadership of Padre R. J. Goodwin it afforded comfort and ministry to the men of units stationed in and around the ruined city. Although its location was precarious, the first wagon-load of furniture was blown up and destroyed before it could be delivered, it remained open for five months before being forced to close. During that time the ground floor served as a canteen and reading room, a cellar, when not in use as a Chapel, was curtained off as a second reading room, and the remainder used as sleeping quarters and a kitchen. By the war's end the premises of Little Talbot House had been destroyed. Rebuilt post-war as the Convent of the Soeurs de Marie and now Instituut Immaculata — a training convent; a wall plaque identifying the site is all that remains.

Within a matter of days of their 1918 spring offensive the Germans had regained virtually all the ground wrested from them the previous autumn and, a little after midnight on 22nd March, several heavy shells landed close to Talbot House. Tubby, lying in bed pondering a course of action, was interrupted by a very agitated Pettifer bursting into the room, shouting: "There's a woman screaming somewhere and I can't a-bear it!" He then rushed downstairs and out of the front door. Tubby jumped out of bed, ushered the staff into the dugout at the rear of the house, and ran out to the street where he saw, less than twenty yards away, a pile of debris that had once been an Officers' Only restaurant. In amongst the wreckage was Pettifer and the house cook. One of the first they rescued was a man wearing only a shirt who was given Tubby's pyjama trousers. Returning to the house, Tubby sent the carpenter across the road to help and then called for Area Provost Marshal Captain Strachan and his men. Of the eleven people in the restaurant, only two survived.

Sat. night, March 23rd 1918 . . . We are having rather a stormy time, but coming through safe and sound, and in the best of spirits and brotherhood. Pettifer distinguished himself greatly last night, and I am trying to get recognition of his gallantry. Today we have been building a real dugout and I have sent the bulk of the staff to sleep away, as they are rather a responsibility.

Easter Monday, April 1st, 1918 . . . You will be delighted to hear Pettifer has got the Military Medal for his gallant rescue of civilians from a house blown down about ten days ago.

At 11.30p.m. on 6th April Tubby received the following signal:

As Poperinghe is out of bounds to all troops it is considered that all furniture should be cleared away and Talbot House closed down. aaa. Are you prepared to open up at another place? aaa. Wire reply. ACG. 2nd Army.

He went to see the Area Provost Marshal and was advised to ignore the signal on the grounds that it was essential the house stay open as everywhere else being closed, troops entering the town might be driven to disorder and that its closure could have an adverse effect on morale. Tubby replied to the Army Chaplain General:

Essential to the morale of the Ypres Salient that Talbot House stay open. Clayton.

He said of the Provost Marshal's response:

"Essential!" It was a strong statement that the APM then made. He had been in Poperinghe for only a few months at most, but he had seen enough to know what the Old House stood for among the men. Not indeed among all men: many thousands who toiled, suffered and died in the Salient never heard the name Talbot House: thousands of others knew it only indirectly by repute. Yet in most units there were one or two men who knew it deeply, and loved it wholeheartedly. Talbot House stood as a sign and a standard not to be surrendered. Many would mark its loss, turn from its closed doors, discouraged and dismayed.

On 11th April Padre Goodwin in Ypres informed Tubby:

Dear Tubby,
Two requests — (i) If we do have to make a sudden

exit a la Shakespeare (alarms without, shouting, they hurry off), what are we to do? Can you raise a promise of a 3-ton lorry from an outer area which could sail in to receive the more valuable things? If so we will hold on to the last gasp and save all we can. If not, shall I burn and smash piano, chairs and all, rather than let Hun have them? Stores we must give away or destroy. Goodie.

On the back of this slip his second request asked Tubby to placate 832 Area Employment Company which had ordered his orderlies back to Poperinghe for kit inspection and renewal. The men were deemed to be in rags and unfit to board a "moving lorry". Another message read:

Tout le monde ayant le vent dessus, and Magrath hoping to have a lorry tomorrow. I am sending my kit and the more valuable articles from the Chapel for a change of air to Poperinghe. They can easily return later if all goes well.

Goodwin and his orderlies arrived at Talbot House at midnight on the 14th, bringing with them "a strange miscellany of secular and sacred salvage". Earlier that day a signal was sent by Poperinghe's Town Major:

Q orders Talbot House be closed at once. Please acknowledge and report the order has been complied with. aaa. DACG, 2 Corps."

Dr. C. J. Magrath, attached to the Y.M.C.A. staff in Ypres, was forced to leave Ypres and billet himself in the house, a move much appreciated by Tubby, busy packing and arranging transport for the house contents. The carpenter's bench had been dismantled and packed in a large canvas sack to be dispatched to safety. Tubby said:

Between us we reorganised the House's work to meet the new conditions. The Chapel was moved downstairs, entrances and cellars were heavily fortified. One shell carried away the stage of the Concert Hall, and two more landed in the garden; a bomb penetrated the water conduit; but the House continued in the greatest happiness to administer comfort, natural and supernatural, to troops still moving through the deserted town. The most valuable fittings had already been removed into safety, thanks to our friends in the Railway Operating Department, so that if the Kaiser had succeeded in reaching the town suddenly for breakfast, according to his announced intention, Talbot House would scarcely have provided him with suitable accommodation.

During these weeks the orders for our closing were frequently repeated, but we put the telescope to the blind eye. To close, when there was still much to be done that there was no one else could do, was a tragedy which only the soul of a hireling could sustain. We took every possible precaution for the safety of our customers, whose gratitude increased as their numbers grew less.

Tubby posted the following notice on the front door of the House:

Although, in obedience to the order of 2nd Corps, the House as a canteen etc., must remain temporarily closed, it also remains the billet of the Garrison Chaplain and of Dr Magrath, who will always be glad to be of any service to any visitors. If the door is shut, the bell on the left is still in the best of working order. P.B.C.

On 16th April he was ordered again to close the house.

Wed. night, April 17th, 1918. Yesterday the House was closed down by order, to-day the APM intervened and lodged a purple protest against my being moved away to other work, my transfer having come through. He was splendid, and I hope has saved me from being shifted, for I should be very sorry to leave yet awhile at least. We have two vans of furniture on the railway, so I can flit at a moments notice if necessary. But don't think the time has come yet, as the House is quite useful still, and more brotherly than ever. We can't safely use the upstairs floors at all, but one ground floor room makes a wonderful little Chapel, and for the rest we can easily cater for our children who are as faithful as ever, and more thankful. Laus Deo.

Since 1916 he had successfully circumvented army regulations. He should have moved to the Somme with the 6th Division and for two years his position had been unclear. He was Army not Corps, a member of the Deputy Assistant Chaplain General's staff attached to 16th Infantry Brigade and, because of this confusion, he was made Garrison Chaplain in April 1918, responsible to the Area Provost Marshal. On 22nd April he wrote:

All very well and fit here, and the Boche quieter. The House is more useful than ever — God bless the old place! — and I have just enough staff to carry on with after a fashion. I am now officially appointed at last to Garrison Chaplain to P. so my flag is nailed to the mast, and j'y suds, j'y reste, which is just what I've been longing for all along.

April 24th ... The place is still going strong, and the Boche still rages furiously. It's all gradually become more uncivilised, shops shut, civilians flee, the Officers' Club closes down. This last is a considerable loss to me, both gastronomically and otherwise. But I've lots of kind friends who give me meals ... folks are thankful TH is still an open door, and my opportunities for spiritual work are great. But of course it's very uncertain how long my garrison chaplaincy will last!

He continued to visit his parishioners throughout the week. Totally fatalistic in his outlook he was undeterred by the increase in enemy shelling. Returning from a parish visit he remarked:

> ... the Boche has knocked down a piece of garden wall. Only a pipsqueak, and no damage even to the rose trees.

While away he was deputised by Dr. Magrath, but both knew the house was existing on borrowed time. The enemy captured Mont Kemmel on 25th April but he and Magrath continued their work in and around the house awaiting the inevitable order to close. In the last three weeks he remained cheerfully optimistic:

> 27th April ... TH may close at any time, but it has done its share and can sing its Nunc Dimittis. Very well and happy myself, thank God. 11th May ... I got leave from the Army to stop here to the last ... The Old House is now alone in its glory, the only open door in the town, and wayfarers are correspondingly thankful. 13th May ... Magrath serves at our Celebrations and plays the organ at our other services ... If the army were as well run as the YM we should be home by now. Please God, I am now to be allowed to stop here and keep the House open till whatever happens, happens. I wish nothing better than this. 15th May ... Corps has just ordered the House to be closed temporarily to troops from today and we can't resist. Probably,

indeed it is wise, but it's hard luck on the wayfarers. Anyhow we've kept the door open longer than anyone else and it's not the Boche that closes it now. Resurget Domus Talbotensis!

Early morning of Whit Monday, 20th May, the final order arrived:

Q insist that you shall vacate Talbot House and seek billet elsewhere. aaa. Please wire acknowledgement and what steps you are taking. DACG. II Corps.

Tubby replied:

In reluctant obedience to this order my billet is hence-forward at Dingley Dell, Hambrock.

A pencil note, added post-war by Tubby reads:

This is the original wire of eviction (May 1918), from Q of 2nd Corps, an ultimatum which brought to a head a series of orders to close down. But the Kaiser failed to reach Poperinghe after all.

Whit Monday, 20th May, 1918, 2p.m. ... We journey to Dingley Dell, a delightful orchard a mile from here, where we have pitched four Armstrong huts. The authorities are determined (quite kindly) that the House should be evacuated now. For a fortnight it has been the only House open in the town; and as the town is now altogether out of bounds, it seems only folly to remain.

We have cleared everything worth having even the electric light fittings; and all the valuables, Chapel furniture, etc., are safely on the train. TH will probably reopen here or elsewhere in a month or so. Meanwhile I shall live happily with Magrath in Dingley Dell, and work round my outside parish more easily than from here. It is in one way of course heart-rending to leave the House. On the other hand, there is nothing for it now to do, and we can sing our Nunc Dimittis with a quiet and thankful heart. We have been wonderfully guarded, guided and blessed; and though many of our children are now at peace, there are many still in this world who have here found Him and been found of Him. Laus Deo.

The following day, Tubby was visited by his cousin, Tom Le Mesurier, then serving with the R.A.F., who was able to lend Tubby his car, enabling him to go in search of a lorry to help his removal. Tubby also received a letter dated 20th May 1918 from the owner of the house:

Monsieur le R. P. Clayton
I have received your valued letter of April 28th from which I took the sum of 300 francs in bank notes for the rent of my house, Rue de l'Hopital at Poperinghe, for the two periods from March 7th to May 7th, 1918. For this I thank you. As I have left

the country to put my family in safety in France, your letter has been forwarded to me at our new address in France. If you are unable to continue to occupy the house, you will oblige me by sending the rent for the ensuing periods to the above address. Receive, Monsieur the Captain, the assurance of my perfect consideration. M. Coevoet."

Tubby added a post-war note to this:

M. Coevoet was (and is — till Toc H can buy its birthplace) the owner of the original House, No. 35, Rue de l'Hopital, Poperinghe. We paid him 150 frs rent a month all through unfailingly, and he then demanded 2,000 frs "degats" for the damage which the Boche had done to it, after the Armistice. Here is a letter of receipt at the most critical period of the war, with the Boche sitting on Kemmel Hill, and Poperinghe "no place for boys".

Two years previously Tubby had written:

Now that the town is so peaceful, the owner is exhibiting a desire to return to his house, so I am in the odd position of having to hope for a little shelling to keep him quiet!

He now hoped that the shelling would cease so that he could stay, but it was not to be, although his exile was to last only four months.

While at La Louvie he devoted his time to conducting services and visiting his parish which now included a number of observation balloon units. He tried to open a new Talbot House in Proven but was vetoed by the authorities. A "mobile House" was established in a box car which travelled up and down the tracks of the back areas.

On 20th September Tubby met a Naval Officer intent on seeing something of the Western Front. In return for a lift Tubby offered himself as a guide and they set off in the direction of Mont Kemmel, now back in British hands. Tubby was horrified by what he saw:

Here Boche were lying everywhere, whole or in bits, shell holes full of them; some glorious French as well and many of those international victims, the transport mules. The tidal wave had come so suddenly and gone with such precipitancy that furniture jutted out from the ruined cottages, and tables still stood laid for meals that were never eaten. Trench warfare did not leave things thus. Grim humour everywhere — German notices and British notices previous and posthumous; a rocking horse without a head on one side of the road and a mule without a head in the opposite ditch.

At the end of the day the two men drove to Poperinghe where they found the Old House dusty but still standing:

... the House front door not being open — still blocked with sandbags — we climbed in through the window, and Pettifer who was down putting things straight, made us tea. Curiously enough my last visitor before the evacuation was also in Navy Blue — dear old Tom Le Mesurier. This was my first visitor in the House again, a good omen for the reopening which will not now, I hope, be very long delayed.

The following week he travelled between La Louvie and Poperinghe refurbishing Talbot House and, on 27th September, equipped with 500 packets of biscuits, he re-occupied the house, reopening it for business on the 30th. From then on, as well as fulfilling his house duties and visiting his parish, he spent much of his time travelling between the Deputy Assistant Chaplain General's office at St. Omer and the Service Ordination Candidates' School at Le Touquet. On 27th October he informed his mother:

M. Coevoet-Camerlynck, the owner wants to come back into the House on November 15th. If so, I think TH will have to be suspended for a month, until we know where we are a bit.

During the first week of November he was approached by the commanding officer of the Railway Construction Company asking him to hold a service for his men the following weekend. Of that weekend he wrote to his father:

... on Saturday afternoon I sallied forth on my 30 miles journey, intending to catch the French return leave train passing through. But as it happened, I was picked up by a lorry running to Wipers, and no sooner did it drop me there, than a French flying tender offered me a lift all the rest of the way. They were carrying some stores, and also a goat, a grandmother, her daughter and two babies. So I climbed in with these and was nearly suffocated. Charitably, we will put it down to the goat; though I have my doubts. Every time one goes across the devastated area, it is more impressive, though already the shell holes are clothed with green, and the industrious Flemish folk are dwelling in pill-boxes. A company of Chinks hold Zonnebeke, and enjoy rushing about in sham affrays, with Boche helmets and rifles. On each side there is a crescendo of desolation. Trees first scarred, then blasted, then stumps, then non-existent. Houses first roofless, then barely recognisable, then pieces of walls with dugouts against or under them, then brick-heaps; then vanished utterly. If you dug you might find bricks, even floors and cellars; but it is wiser not to. For the rest, wire all rusted and tangled, rotting sandbags, broken wheels, piles of unused shells, boxes of ammunition, timber for the roads, duckboard tracks, grotesque direction posts in two tongues, dead mules flung into inadequate shell holes go on in one huge nightmare across the rise and fall of the ground. Here and there rough crosses still stand, but most in the vortex have been blotted out.

The clearance of this ground is already proceeding in various ways, it will be years before it resembles anything normal ... but the pill-boxes and the tanks will always stay, unless blown up which would be sacrilege. The tanks — there must be quite a hundred altogether — are the most eerie things of all; riddled with explosives, they retain not only their outline with its peculiar menace, but the exact position in which they met their death. They seem like monsters of the iron age, frozen in the act of springing. However, I mustn't loiter in no man's land any longer.

Behold us then emerging in looking-glass land ... the fields grow recognisable, the houses merely uninhabitable, and the road merely vile. This ground was rushed in the advance, so it has suffered only slightly by comparison, and the graves are scattered and isolated. The great defence line here still stands — it was never held, or it could have been held for ever; but cannon fodder was too strictly rationed by then.

We turn into the broad highway from Menin to Roulers. After 3 or 4 kilos along here, I reach my nearest point and drop off, complete with thermos flask, biscuits, etc. (food is scarce up there), and my Church essentials including Uncle Ernest's Communion set. I walk to the train which is construction HQ, and have a riotous late tea in the old Boche van which is their mess, and hear all the news. Five out of seven officers are keen communicants, as I know of old; but tomorrow it can't be. Late evening service after the day's work is the most that may be this Sunday. All the Companies are racing against time too with their particular parts of the line. So I decide to join one of the reconnaissance parties on the morrow, and am accepted.

Breakfast at 7.30 and start in box car at 8, with survey party on the southern line. Renaise is one objective, but fighting is still going on, and yesterday the Boche still held the Scheldt, where he had another unassailable position, with a broad stream in front, and a hill 5 times Kemmel for observation. Now, who knows? He is said to be in full retreat. The infantry have crossed and found no trace of him. As we approach the Scheldt, signs of desperate fighting and whirlwind shelling are painfully recent. One village is almost Wiperesque; and Avelgem lying on one side of the stream is as though a tornado had struck it. Here we can go no further by road, for the bridges are down. Leaving the wreckage of the station, we pick our way along the line which is on a steep embankment. This has been mined and blown every 100 feet or so, and there may be more still beneath. Only too obviously, the infantry came this way yesterday. Suddenly the line stops in nothingness. Bridge No. 1 has gone, but 100 yards up stream there is a gang plank bridge resting on the invaluable petrol tin floats. By this we cross and find ourselves in the Boche front line, still warm with him as it were. Only the officer comes after me. We go on together, the two of us.

It looks as if something else would soon happen inside the buttress on the further bank. Anyhow, there's a chamber there in the side of it, with some sticks of chocolate stuff that we leave severely alone. I wander on ahead, and find some Belgians wringing their hands at the door of a cottage beside the line. The Boche have taken everything, and smashed the rest; there was much rifle fire here yesterday, and their garden is full of hand grenades. Will Monsieur move them? I select a Mill's bomb, which looks homely, and rid them of that at least. How it got there I don't know. The rest is Boche stuff with wooden handles, and I suggest the digging of a large "trou" in the field, which they approve. I give them 2d of biscuits and pass on, as the OC has overtaken me. So along for half a mile — no signs of anyone, Boche or British; except for one plane, equally lost apparently, overhead. Every level crossing has been blown up with buried Minenwerfers, and at one a big pile of them remains apparently unused. But we don't investigate. Yesterday the Boche went along here for the last time.

At the remains of the next station we sit down. It is a heavenly day. Resuming our march, we come to a railwayman's cottage. Outside are two small girls. I offer them chocolate, but they run indoors shyly. The door is opened by their father, who welcomes me in with rejoicing. Their mother is making a savoury dish of horsemeat from a horse killed nearby. It is the first meat meal, they assure me, that they have had for two years! I leave them to their Sunday dinner ... we turn off two miles on and come back by road. It is longer, but it's worth it: for now we meet our own folk in all their glory. Infantry pouring through, with their bands playing them along. Not a gorgeous military spectacle, for they are all tired. But all along the road the villages are out to welcome and to wonder. The bands play everything and anything to keep them going. The men, weary though they are, put their thumbs in their packstraps, and step out well. Those that have no bands, whistle or sing snatches. They do not look proud, but infinitely patient, and kindly, and domestic, and with all there's a little twinkle in their eyes. I see some old friends among them, but they are mostly the younger brothers. Most of my generation lie quietly asleep with the tanks keeping guard over their slumbers.

Talbot House remained open until Christmas 1918 when virtually all its contents were packed and shipped to England. Maurice Coevoet returned in late January 1919, and at a formal gathering on 6th February the keys to the house were handed over to him by Tubby and Neville Talbot.

# CHAPTER
# TEN

# The Peace of Flanders

I am the light of the world: he that followeth me shall
not walk in the darkness, but shall have the light of
life.

*John VIII.12*

As early as 1917 Tubby and a group of colleagues had
discussed the feasibility of establishing a club in London
to carry on the 1st traditions of the house, a Talbot
House UK. Between 1915 and 1918 some 25,000 men
took Holy Communion in Talbot House and many
thousands of them filled in the Communicant Roll
Forms, which always lay ready for completion on the
billiard table at the foot of the Chapel stairs. Shortly
after the Armistice the Service Ordination Candidates'
lists had outgrown Tubby's personal capabilities and
were transferred to the Headquarters of Bishop Gwynne
in London. Here, working in conjunction with the
Defence Staffs, plans were set in motion for the early
demobilisation and collection of all candidates, and the
setting up of two Ordination Test Schools in France.

Encouraged by the response to contacts made through
the Communion Rolls and the considerable success he

was having tracing other old friends Tubby and an article in the *St. Martin's Messenger*, a parish periodical run by his cousin Dick Sheppard, Vicar of St. Martin-in-the-Fields, detailing plans for a rebirth of Talbot House in London:

Depose Nelson, remove the column, ungum the lions, deduct the fountains, wash out the National Gallery, and cease to visualise Whitehall; then roll the surface flat (except for execrable pave) and, with these trifling alterations, Trafalgar Square becomes the Grande Place of Poperinghe. You must also, by the way, rebuild St. Martin's, and put a shellhole through its tower, and a clock that declares for years on end that it is half past five, thus reminding us of human fallibility in high quarters.

The real similarity between the two places is, however, more readily realisable, for Poperinghe Square was for four years to the BEF what Trafalgar Square is to London — a big place through which well-nigh every man must pass on his pilgrimage; an open place wherein he takes his first or last intermediate breather before getting to or from business; near enough to the scene of work to warrant and provoke a pause; remote enough to make a pause a pleasure reasonably immune from accident.

What is to happen to the place that meant so much to so many? The fellowship of Talbot House is a fellowship far too great to lose. It is my design to find quarters in London where that fellowship can be made to rise like a Phoenix and flourish once again.

The only great fault I find, as a parson, with London, is that there aren't nearly enough public houses in the place. There are places so-called, no doubt, but they are tied to one tradition as well as to one brewery. The innkeepers are all too humble to approach you or too proud to be approached. Where is the bustling Boniface of literature? He is bedimmed by a guinea-pig directorate; he is dehumanised by the shadow of shares-cum-dividends.

Our fancy leads us to a cosy house with a good ABC downstairs; and upstairs, lecture room, library, games rooms, and "grousing" rooms, together with a London Territorial Lethe chamber, where warlike reminiscences may merge wholly into imaginative art; in short, a junior Cavendish Club, though not quite so serious; its membership (at 10/- shall we say?) would be the 4,000 already on the Communicants' Roll of the Old House (of whom some 500 are in London), reinforced from the Civil Service and Territorial World — a class who, among the faithless, were surprisingly faithful to Mother Church, in reverse ratio, perhaps, to the care she bestowed on them.

An inn without beds is like a song without a chorus, therefore we must have a hostel in our hostelry; for in London men are even more homeless than they were in Flanders. The only financial detail yet decided upon is that, when the water-rate question becomes acute, we are going to draw water in a dixie from the fountains of the Square. You see, we are practical prophets, and the smallest detail is thus completely envisaged.

All this is not yet . . . Meanwhile, will St. Martin cover the beggar with its ample cloak, and seek God's will concerning Talbot House in town?

In 1915 the church had equally envisaged the need for an expansion of its clergy to be recruited from all ranks of the services after the cessation of hostilities. In 1916, supporting this need, Tubby posted a notice:

Ordination Candidates
It is not known widely enough among Churchmen in the Army that the Church at home has adopted a great plan whereby to add to her Ministry after the war a great body of the best men from the Army and Navy, irrespective of their financial to meet the cost of their training.

Already under this scheme, over 1,400 candidates for Ordination have come forward from all ranks and all fronts: 150 of these have been enrolled in Talbot House. I shall be glad to get in touch with any further candidates, and to explain the scheme to any inquirers. P.B. Clayton.

A pencil note added to the original of the above explains: that it was a 1918 amended notice of the version posted in 1916.

Between 1919 and 1922, Tubby, as the St. Mary's curate, was seconded to the staff of the Knutsford Test School. During this period he spent very little time there. Following the favourable response to the Communication Roll contact, the article in the "St. Martin's Messenger" and the publication of his *Tales of Talbot House* in September 1919, he regularly commuted to and from London. Whilst in the capital he based himself in his sister's flat where a steady stream of visitors flowed every day forming the embryo that would develop into Toc H. Nearly 800 old friends, including 200 ex-officers, had expressed a desire to assist Tubby's quest. On 8th November he drew up an agenda for a meeting to be held at the Central Church Fund Office, Westminster, on the 15th. Worded in a manner reminiscent of the old Notice Board it read:

Operation Order No. 1.
Assembly Point: Central Church Fund Office,
40, Great Smith Street,
Map Ref. SW1. Westminster.

Z.Day: Saturday, 15th November, 1919.

Zero hour: 15.00 (3p.m.)

I. Information; The attack on the problem of re-opening Talbot House will be carried out by a Round Table Conference thirty in number, troops being drawn from Talbotousians past, present, and to come. The attack will be covered by a creeping barrage of business advisors supported by expert Londoners. A Section of Clerical Tanks will co-operate. The operations will be under the direction of Gen. R.S. May, CMG, DSO, etc.

II. Intentions.

(i) The Minutes of the First Meeting

(ii) Correspondence from the forward dump

(iii) Report on the second edition of the book

(iv) Report on membership

(v) Report on House reconnaissance party

(vi) Report on suggested liaison work

(vii) Financial situation and prospects

(viii) Consideration of draft Appeal

III. Methods of Advance: When the blue line is reached and consolidated tea will be taken, before the supports pass through and capture the green line.

IV. Nature of Country:

The vital need of maintaining the old fellowship and extending it to the younger clerks, civil servants and students of London offers special opportunity for the initiative of all arms, and risks must be boldly taken.

The outcome of this meeting was threefold:- firstly, due to there existing in London a Talbot Society, he used the army signalese for Talbot House thus forming the Toc H Movement.

A Central Executive Committee was created as follows:

Presidents:
His Grace The Archbishop of Canterbury.
Field Marshal Lord Plumer, GCB, GCMG, GCVO.
Vice Presidents:
The Earl of Cavan, KP, GCMG, KCB, MVO.
The Countess Grosvenor.
Committee:
Major-General R.S. May, CB, CMG, DSO.
    (Chairman).
Lieutenant-Colonel A.S. Bates, DSO, TD.
I. Hamilton Benn, Esq., CB, DSO, MP.
W.J.M. Burton, Esq.
Lady Byng of Vimy.
Sir Francis Dent.
Montague Ellis, Esq.
Sir Alfred Pearce Gould, KCVO, CBE.
J. Manclark Hollis, Esq.
Lieutenant-General Sir Aylmer Hunter-Weston,
    KCB, DSO, MP.
General Hon. Sir Herbert Alexander Lawrence,
    KCB.
Reverend Prebendary F. Partridge.
Alexander Paterson, Esq.
Lady Phillimore.

Colonel Lord Saye And Sele.
Reverend H.R.L. Sheppard, MA.
H. Shiner, Esq., DSO, MC.
Reverend Neville S. Talbot, MC.
Trevelyan Thompson, Esq., MP.
Founder Padre; P. B. Clayton.

It was agreed that the fellowship of Talbot House should be preserved and further developed to embrace a younger membership.

At about the same time that the Toc H Movement was born Tubby moved into an apartment at 36, St. George's Mansions, London which he shared with Herbert Shiner; Frank Wilkins, Arthur Pettifer, and George Spragg, a Shakespearian actor. Once the whereabouts of Tubby became known visitors flocked to the flat to renew old acquaintances and rekindle the fellowship of Talbot House. Tubby used many means to let his whereabouts be known, but in Red Lion Square a simple note fixed to a long bell pull proved most effective:

Toc H. the REV. P. B. CLAYTON, formerly of POPERINGHE and YPRES.

Talbot House moved to Queen's Gate Gardens in early 1920 becoming known as Toc H. Mark I. Within six months, so great was the flow of guests and demands on its amenities, it became obvious that new premises were needed. In less than twelve months 1,600 had visited the flat and 400 found overnight accommodation there. Another house, for Toc H Mark II, was provided by the Duke of Westminster in St. George's Square, Pimlico, followed later by the gift of the adjoining property.

The Toc H Movement was not confined to London; by the end of 1920 there were Houses in Edinburgh, Newcastle, Durham, Poole, Manchester, Stockport, Liverpool, Birkenhead, Birmingham, Leeds, Sheffield, Portsmouth, Gosport, Maidstone, Brighton, Northampton, Swindon, Bristol, Cheltenham, Worcester, Oxford, Cambridge, Saffron Walden and High Wycombe. By January 1921 there were seventy of them throughout the UK as well as fellowship branches in factories and workshops. In London a further two houses opened. Tubby was delighted and wrote:

Every big thing was little at its birth. Britain is littered with Societies, but only God can make a family.

During 1921 Toc H expanded rapidly, and the strain began to tell on Tubby. Hearing of this, his old friend, Lord Byng of Vimy, in his capacity as Governor General of Canada, invited Tubby to visit Ottawa to give a series of lectures. Archbishop Davidson, in turn, sent him to see Sir George and Lady Parkin, in Chelsea. Meeting their daughter, Alice, wife of the Canadian statesman Vincent Massey, resulted in Tubby being given letters of introduction to the well known and influential of Canada. Between 15th January 1922, and his return to England at the end of March, Tubby carried out a gruelling non-stop tour of lectures and meetings throughout Canada and the Northern United States. He laid the foundations for Toc H in both countries, and netted a considerable sum of money for the Movement in the process. This was to be the first of many tours Tubby would undertake.

In July 1922 he was summoned to the bedside of the then sick Archbishop Randall Davidson at Lambeth Palace, who enquired about Knutsford and the recently opened Talbot House Mark II and Toc H. offering assistance in whatever capacity he could. He mentioned that, whilst visiting Tower Hill he had found the Church of All Hallows-by-the-Tower "closed, cold and neglected," and in desperate need of a vicar. Tubby, somewhat taken aback by what was clearly the offer of the vicarage, pleaded that Toc H was now his life's work. The Archbishop merely nodded and requested he go away to pray and meditate on the proposal. Tubby did as he was asked, and also went along to inspect the Church:

The walls were streaked with grime, floor boards agape, the rats were moving to and fro among them; the windows were almost opaque with soot; electric lights in niggardly quantity only rendered visible the darkness and unrelieved decay. The Church had been almost disused for months, and little visited for many years.

On 11th August the Archbishop wrote, officially offering him All Hallows:

After much meditation, much consultation, many criticisms, and I need hardly say earnest prayers, I write to suggest that you should let me nominate you to the Vicarage of All Hallows, Barking, with the view to your making that historic Church a centre for work among the clerks and others in the City whom you can gather into the company of those for whose deepest welfare you cater, and whom you have shown yourself capable of helping. I do not ask you to let it be all (possibly not even chiefly as the years run on) Toc H work. I want you to have a free hand to use whatever means God seems to show you to be the best for winning these young fellows to Christ. All Hallows is the very place either as a centre for Foreign Ministry work or as a centre for Home Mission work in London. I therefore have no difficulties about finding a good man for a great position.

November 1922 saw Philip Clayton, co-Founder Padre, Talbot House, Poperinghe and Ypres; innovator and staff member, Service Candidates Test School, Le Touquet and Knutsford; Founder Padre of Toc H; former curate of St. Mary's Church, Portsea, now Vicar of All Hallows-by-the-Tower, London, a position he held for 40 years.

During the Great War many thousands of other men and women experienced the fellowship of Talbot House, breaking down barriers that separated rank and social order. Whether in the privacy of the Chaplain's Room, or in an Upper Room congregation, these men repeatedly pledged their faith in God. In Talbot House they found a shared Peace, a state of mind from which they drew the strength to overcome the enduring pain and suffering of the salient. They pledged their faith in their fellow man, sharing strengths and weaknesses, that they might better serve each other. Those who visited Talbot House were only men — their common prayer — to survive where survival depended on miracles. Miracles were in short supply and demanded a heavy premium in the Ypres Salient. It is not unrealistic to say that a combination of faith, prayer and miracles saw many of them, and others, safely through to the end of the war. But, a deciding factor in many cases was fellowship, the brotherhood of man.

They came together after the war because they believed their fellowship should continue to serve their fellow man. They had known and been aided by the Peace of Flanders — through Toc H they were determined the Peace would serve others.

Within five years of the re-birth of Talbot House in 1919, the Movement could be found all round the globe. Sometimes there were strong branches in the main cities and centres, sometimes a branch would spring up surprisingly in some lonely and remote spot, sometimes there would just be a cor-respondent, ready to welcome travellers along the business routes of the world. This erratic kind of development was the result of the way men are taken to every country by their business in life. Members who had been at the Old House were to be found in many countries, in India and the East, in North and South America, in Asia and Africa, and where they went Toc H seed took root and as often as not, flourished. It was very much like the seeds of willow herb and thistledown which the winds carried into the nooks and crannies of bombed London after the last war, and which there bloomed acceptably, transfiguring ugliness into beauty.

Alison B.S. Macfie.

# CHAPTER
# ELEVEN

# A Piece of Flanders

Many hands make light work
*Proverb*

With high numbers of ex-servicemen and bereaved families visiting the battlefields of Flanders, Toc H published the book *A Pilgrims Guide to the Ypres Salient*. Written and compiled entirely by ex-servicemen, it contains 91 pages of information including suggested tours and a guide to the cemeteries. It also featured a number of eyewitness accounts on life in the Salient during the war. It was published to raise funds for "the maintenance of Talbot House in London" for which the sum of £30,000 was being sought.

A great number of the visitors made their way to Poperinghe and Talbot House and, within weeks of re-occupying it, Mr Coevoet's privacy was imposed upon by a succession of predominantly British visitors accompanied by friends, sweethearts, wives, and families, all wishing to visit his house. Allegedly, Mr Coevoet came downstairs for breakfast once to find British visitors asleep on the floor of his hall. At other times he found people wandering about the house and in the garden. Story has it that his wife awoke to find two British visitors in her bedroom. The shell-damaged garden wall gave easy access and the rear doors were never locked. Although not intended to be taken literally, a sign on the Franco-Belgian border compounded the problem with its "Visit Talbot House" message.

From the moment the Great War ended Tubby had two grand designs in life. One was to see Talbot House continue its good work and Christian fellowship in London, the other, to secure the purchase of the original Old House in Poperinghe. Between 1919 and 1927 he was fully occupied with the expansion of the Toc H Movement, touring extensively worldwide to further its growth abroad. He spent little time in the UK during this period but it was always his intention to return to his beloved Poperinghe to follow up his ambition to buy the property which saw the birth of the movement.

He felt the association between thousands of men and Talbot House should continue, but the house-owner, had rapidly become un-cooperative towards the crowds of visitors. He refused to allow a plaque to be placed on the walls of his home and any hopes that Tubby had were fast diminishing. By mid 1924, the situation for him proved intolerable, on 12th August, he wrote to HRH The Prince of Wales:

It is a great hope among many of us that we may ultimately be able to purchase at a fair price the old house in Poperinghe and keep it for our pilgrims and re-establish its Chapel, which would in many ways be the most perfect Church for the Salient, as suggested by Lord French. Meanwhile we would earnestly ask that Monsieur Coevoet-Camerlynck should not be so inhospitable to pilgrims who desire the privilege of entrance.

After a great deal of consultation and correspondence, Mr Coevoet remained adamant in his refusal to admit pilgrims to enter his house, let alone discuss the sale of it. In 1926 Tubby, armed with a personal letter of introduction from Prince de Croye, of the Belgian Embassy in London, to the Burgomaster of Poperinghe, led the first official Toc H Pilgrimage to Flanders. The Burgomaster, successfully pleading the cause of the pilgrims to Mr Coevoet, secured entrance for them in groups of twenty. Jock Gillespie, one of the pilgrims recalled:

Tubby celebrated next morning at the Great Stone of Remembrance in the Reservoir Cemetery at Ypres. Most of the main body went to Poperinghe by train and the women by bus. This time the doors were open and Tubby went in with the first twenty people to the Chapel. The rest of us, awaiting our turn, went round the garden with the "Gen". The brick wall on the left was still pock-marked by shell-fire. "Gee" took us across the garden and showed us where the Carpenters bench was found. Finally it was our turn to go upstairs. As we mounted the narrow stairway we met the first party coming down and we saw by their faces that they had not only seen, but also had understood their vision. The loft had retained its use as an attic but at one end still stood the dais that had supported the Carpenters bench and there, in front of this, stood Tubby with bowed head; a disused pram stood in one corner and some onions were laid out on the floor. All instinctively knelt as we entered for we knew that the ground whereon we stood was holy.

This first pilgrimage paved the way for many others over the following years. Henry Williamson visited in 1927 and, without asking, was both cordially welcomed and escorted to the chapel.

In 1926, commemorating the tenth anniversary of the First Day of the Somme, the Barking Corn Exchange organised a ceremony in memory of fellow Londoners who had fallen on that fateful day. Tubby, as vicar at All Hallows, was invited to officiate. Invitations were hurriedly dispatched to all surviving next of kin, ex-servicemen, British Legion and local associations, the heads of City commerce and businessmen and a telegram was sent to Sir Charles Wakefield, Chairman of a company which dealt in lubricating oils and appliances.

After the ceremony Tubby introduced himself to Sir Charles and discussed, amongst other things, his plans for the renovation of both All Hallows and Tower Hill. Wakefield, he had been the Lord Mayor in 1915, was a known benefactor of military charitable causes and, impressed by Tubby's ideas, pledged his support. During their discourse they were joined by Major Paul Slessor and there began a friendship that would endure for the remainder of their lives.

Between 1926 and 1929 Lord Wakefield, through personal correspondence with Mr Coevoet, bought the property himself, donating it to the Toc H movement. The purchase was handled for him by Major Paul Slessor who finalised it on 20th December 1929.

On 5th April 1931, the House was officially inaugurated with Lord Wakefield, Major Slessor, Tubby Clayton and a multitude of members of the Toc H movement attending the ceremony.

To enable the needy to visit, a subsidy of £250 per annum was required, as was a permanent housekeeper, and a number of alterations were needed to the house itself. Lord Wakefield took it upon himself to pay for whatever repairs and alterations were required and provided an endowment of £10,000 for its upkeep.

All this is an immense task which may be of the widest influence on English life and character. There are now, as you know, nearly two hundred schools in touch with Toc H and these boys must have facts presented to them in every way that is wise and serviceable. Through my experience already of introducing parties of schoolboys to the Old House and the surrounding country, I am quite certain that the kind of plan which I have sketched above is virtually essential to the full use of this inheritance.

The Reverend J.R. Lewis visited in the spring of 1931 and wrote to Tubby:

I find it very difficult to describe in any way the impression that the Old House gave to me, save only that it was something unique. I learned for the first time how a place can be peopled with Spirits of the Past. Throughout the House, but especially in the Upper Room, I was just aware of the presence of the Elder Brethren — a strange, quite unique, but very real experience. And if this was what I felt, who am new to Toc H and never fought in the war, I can but dimly guess what the House means to Toc H as a whole and to you especially who knew it in the war years. The glimpse that I was able to catch of the spirit that is at the heart of Toc H in the gatherings we had together is something that I prize immensely, not only because it helped me to a knowledge of the movement which I am entering, but because it sounded again to me personally that note of devotion to service to our Lord which is the way of my Ministry.

An ex-Sapper, Will Leonard also wrote:

On arrival at Talbot House, Poperinghe, I took the first opportunity possible, and kneeled down in the Upper Room. I don't remember praying or using any words, I may have done; but I remember (as I had done some weeks previously) asking God for an answer to some problem which was worrying

me at Easter time 1917. Then, all unbidden, there
came into my mind the lines from The Ancient
Mariner (which I had not read for years).

> The many men, so beautiful!
> And they all dead did lie.
> And a thousand thousand slimy things
> Lived on, and so did I.

I remembered what you wrote just after the war,
about the best men having died and left us
second-raters to carry on the jobs and do the things
they would have tried to do had they lived. I felt
greatly abashed. My mind didn't wander as much
as usual, and I became more absorbed in the
service than any time for some years. I can
remember kneeling down again after the reception,
so what happened must have been after that. I think
then my mind was as near passive as ever I get in
church. I don't usually think in pictures; but then,
there came into my mind a vision, as if I stood on
high ground looking back from the Line, over a
long stretch of desolate, muddy, rain swept country,
dimly seeing figures moving. In short, just such a
scene as we were familiar enough with in the war
years; but with this difference, that much more
poignantly than I ever did in the war years I felt
something of the almost intolerable and seemingly
interminable agony of it. (And then suddenly the
vision vanished.) I then found it hard to remain
kneeling. I think I half rose and kneeled again; but

I felt impelled to stand up and when I did (though I saw no vision and was fully conscious of where I was and what I was doing), I felt that I was standing in the presence of a great company of men, free through Christ, and in some way their agony linked up with His. I think I remained standing, conscious of their presence, all the time to the end of the service, when I knelt down, here was the sense of being uplifted in that Great Company, my unworthiness to be of their company eliminated; but what, I think, shook me was the realisation, in some measure, of the agony they had known.

*We go back to our beginnings to understand our growth. The Old House is more than a place of sentiment — it is a fact of history. I know fellows of straight and simple mind who have found the depths of Toc H in no crowded Guest Nights but in the strange simplicity of a Belgian house where it all began.*

Alec Paterson

Note:
In October 1996 the Talbot House Association purchased the old hop-store Concert Hall adjacent to the garden of Talbot House and plans through its acquisition to further develop its ties with the local community and encourage the local youth to become actively involved in the "living museum" that is Talbot House today.

# CHAPTER
# TWELVE

# World War Two

I believe it is Peace for our time.
*Prime Minister, Neville Chamberlain.*
*30th September 1938.*

A little over twenty years after the Armistice the flames of war raged uncontrollably across Europe once again, ignited by Germany's violation of Poland. A B.B.C. War Correspondent, Frank Gillard, a schoolmaster prior to the outbreak of the Second World War, was also a member of Toc H:

Toc H was maintaining the Old House in Pop... and large numbers of visitors ... some were old soldiers who came back to revive memories of the war and some were relatives of men who'd lost their lives in the war. It was looked after by a resident Belgian couple, dear people, sweet people, but always with a senior Toc H person there ... as part of my work for Toc H I went over for a month or so in the summer in order to be the temporary warden of Talbot House, receive the guests and take them out and let them have a look at the trenches and some of the relics of World War I as they still existed in that Flanders area. I was there doing this warden job in 1939 in the weeks immediately before the outbreak of the Second World War and we had a great flow of visitors coming to Talbot House that summer season. One of them was a leading member of Parliament called Mather and as we toured the garden and sat down over coffee I said to him that I was pretty anxious about the international situation . . . it looked to be building up in a very threatening way. I wondered if it was wise in my staying on. I thought that war was probably imminent, whether it would be safe to get away . . . he said to me "You needn't have the slightest concern about that Mr Gillard," he said "there isn't going to be any war at all. I assure you, war is not going to break out." Well two weeks after that Hitler was pushing his armies into Poland . . . I just got out . . . my connection with Talbot House ran right up to the outbreak of World War Two.

As the British Army retreated towards Dunkirk during mid and late May 1940, Poperinghe witnessed scenes reminiscent of its Great War garrison days as thousands of soldiers passed through the narrow streets and Talbot House once again catered, albeit briefly, to their needs both spiritual and recreational.

Poperinghe became something of a recreation centre for German troops in the area. During the first two or three weeks of occupation Talbot House was used as a billet for Austrian troops much to the chagrin of the caretakers Rene and Alida Berat. Although they stole all the bedding upon departure, whilst they were on the premises they took great care not to misbehave and never touched any of the artifacts. After their departure the House remained virtually unnoticed by the invader and it was a few weeks before they showed further interest.

Fortunately for Talbot House, an influential person in Poperinghe at that time was Arthur Lahaye, a lawyer by profession, he later became a Judge and town Burgomaster and the Secretary to the Talbot House Association. Having been temporarily interned with the local dignitaries and intelligentsia, he was released and returned to Popcringhc. One of the first acts he performed was the convening of an Extra Ordinary General Meeting for the local Association members in order that protective measures for the House could be taken.

Due to the activities of a Belgian collaborator the true significance of Talbot House and what it stood for was known to the enemy and it was singled-out for particularly close attention by the German Commandant of Ghent. It was his belief Talbot House was not only British, but the meeting place of a subversive enemy group known as Toc H.

The Talbot House Association managed to convince the Germans that Toc H was a Belgian Society and the sole proprietor of the house and its contents. In the meantime, a local association, Friends of the Old House, had taken the precaution of emptying it of its more valuable contents.

In 1941 the local German Commanding Officer requisitioned and occupied it himself, but not before it was stripped of the rest of its contents, which were hidden throughout the town, by members of the Friends of the Old House. The only item left was Major Paul Slessor's trilby hat which was left hanging on the back of the office door.

When the Commanding Officer found it empty he was furious. Feigning ignorance Arthur Lahaye is alleged to have replied, "You said nothing about the contents when you requisitioned the house. I can only assume that needy locals must have helped themselves."

Paul Slessor had already transported Tubby's chapel vessels to London where they can be found today, on display in the undercroft of All Hallows.

The carved stone head of a cherub, found in the organ loft in the ruins of St. Martin's cathedral in Ypres was another artefact that was hidden during the Second World War and thought to have been lost for ever. It was retrieved in 1983 when the house warden, digging at the foot of the monkey-puzzle tree in the garden, struck what was at first thought to be a large rock, but turned out to be the head of the cherub. It now hangs on a wall on the first floor of the house.

... the last surviving head of a series of marble heads that once graced the organ loft of St. Martin's Cathedral, Ypres, secured by the RE's for Talbot House.

Until its requisition in 1941 the house served as a billet for soldiers from units in the vicinity. In the late summer of 1941 it became a brothel, when a contingent of Navy Girls was installed to meet the physical needs of the local German officers.

On Wednesday, 6th September 1944, Poperinghe was officially declared "liberated" by General Maczek's 3rd Polish Armoured Division. Immediately prior to the hurried departure of the Germans from Talbot House the staff of General Von Runstedt, the occupant at the time, made a large bonfire on the floor of the conservatory in an attempt to destroy files and documents. Such was the hurried departure of the enemy that as they exited from the front of the House so, two local people rushed in from the rear and extinguished the fire.

We pulled up outside the front door of the Old House. A great Union Jack was hanging from an upper window. The place badly needed a coat of paint, but otherwise it was in excellent condition. Not a pane of glass was broken. The big front door swung open, and there, in the entrance hall, stood a reception committee — armed members of the Belgian Resistance Movement who were standing guard over this piece of British property. I did a quick tour of the House. All the furnishings were unfamiliar, but they were good. The Germans living there had certainly made themselves comfortable. The remains of their last meal lay on the table in Tubby's room overlooking the gardens on the first floor, which had been their mess. The bedrooms were littered with odd bits of property — personal property — which they had not had time to collect together. On the second floor landing the Lamp, of course, was missing, and the carving of the Last Supper had gone from the panelled wall. The large room on the west side of this landing (surely it had used to be one large room — the Lounge — or is my memory playing tricks?) had been divided into two by a partition of lath and plaster.

The stairway door to the Upper Room stood open. Upstairs was all the familiar Chapel furniture, stacked away in the corner — the harmonium and everything, all intact as far as I could see. The room had just been dismantled (probably before the German occupation) and left.

In the garden Paul Slessor's waterworks were dirty but completely preserved. One week of hard work by half a dozen willing cleaners and the whole place will be as immaculate as ever.

The foregoing account by Frank Gillard was received on 19th September, supposedly twelve days after he wrote it. It was more likely written on 16th or 17th which would explain the anomalies in the text. The Lounge was on the first floor landing, the waterworks had been damaged by explosives, and the Chapel fittings were not returned until either the 17th or 18th at the earliest.

At 5.30p.m., Thursday, 7th September 1944, the B.B.C. broadcast:

Hello B.B.C.! This is Frank Gillard in Northern Belgium. We came to Poperinghe, a name that will bring back memories to hundreds of thousands of fighting men of those days. I'm glad to bring the news that Talbot House in Poperinghe which was a home from home for our troops in the last war, and which was the birthplace of Toc H. Talbot House stands intact, with scarcely a pane of glass broken. The Germans that were living in the house left at such speed that a half eaten meal still lay on the table this morning. Talbot House is British property and this morning armed Belgians were standing guard over it.

Flying Officer James Huggins, 2757 Squadron Royal Air Force:

On the 13th September, I, in company with a flight of armoured fighting vehicles of the Royal Air Force Regiment, entered Poperinghe for purposes military. Requiring accommodation for both men and vehicles, we visited the Burgomaster. He suggested we occupy Talbot House, as it was most suited to our needs. On entering Talbot House we found that the Germans had committed a crime equal to sacrilege; the interior was in a disgusting condition and the whole place so altered as to pass recognition. There were a few occupants, Belgian

Patriots, members of an organisation similar to our fire-watchers, but these people had only been in occupation for a few days. However, with the little time at our disposal we endeavoured to restore where possible, and, with the help of a Canadian chaplain, the Chapel took on the semblance of sanctity.

On 15th September Padre E.C. Royle, 1st Battalion, Black Watch of Canada, wrote:

I have been down to Pop. I arranged a table and a few chairs, with cross and candle sticks on the table, as an effort to re-capture the atmosphere of the Upper Room. This will do as a temporary measure until the carefully hidden furnishings can be brought out and restored to their rightful place. There is a small but steady stream of pilgrims to the House, and they all climb to the Upper Room; I felt the cross, etc., would give them the invitation to kneel and pray.

Immediately prior to the outbreak of the Second World War until the requisition, Rene and Alida Berat had been resident caretakers at the house.

Tubby received a Red Cross message, dated 25th April 1944:

Rene dead. I very unfortunate, alone in the world. Glad to have news. Always thinking of you and all the friends, also Paul. Compliments to all friends. Alida.

Frank Gillard had known the Berats in 1939:

But what of Rene and Alida? Madame? — "Nix!" was all I could get out of the Belgian guards. So I dashed across the street to the Boulangerie, where the good wife, after working out her excitement upon me, told me that Monsieur was mort but that Madame was now in the Hopital Sacre Coeur.

I forced my way through the crowds in the Square — past the lines of collaborators still being marched into the Hotel de Ville by the patriots and walked right in through the front door of the Old Folks' Building. A Sister led me to the door of Alida's room. She was sitting all alone on a high chair at a little table by the window eating her mid-day meal. My hasty entry was a great shock to her. I should have been announced. For a moment she was speechless. Then she was weeping on my shoulder. Her first words were "Rene — he is dead."

Five minutes later she had completely recovered herself, and was her own lively self again, telling how she had protected Talbot House against the Germans. How she had rebuked them when they spilt water on the floors, or left the wash house dirty. She and Rene had longed for our return. It became an obsession with Rene — everyday he would gaze towards the Channel — "Will they never come?" He had two strokes but recovered. They moved into the Sacre Coeur, where he could have proper care. Then, five months ago, Rene had had his third stroke, and in the afternoon it was all over.

All the more precious belongings of the House, she told me, were in safe keeping. Some were in the care of members of the Association.

She asked eagerly after all her old friends. She had been hearing regularly, in quite a different way, from me, for tucked away in a dark corner of her room she had a radio set on which she had listened daily to London despite the Nazi ban.

Alida now lives for the day when Toc H men and women will return to Poperinghe. She herself has enough money and is reasonably comfortable and well cared for. When I left her the rain had ceased and she was putting on her clothes, getting ready to pay her first post-liberation visit to the Old House. With all her widowhood and her seventy years her loyalty remains as ever.

Throughout the occupation of Poperinghe a number of wild rumours circulated in the UK with regard to the Old House. One of these was the SS Headquarters story, another said the House had been damaged/destroyed by enemy bombing. Indeed, as early as 1940, Staff Sergeant L. C. Waldron, in the retreat to Dunkirk reported: "I passed through Pop on May 28th/29th. The Old House was still then burning and we could not stay."

Another story went so far as to state that the House had been deliberately demolished after having been thoroughly looted and all manner of depraved acts committed in the chapel. Tubby would not have been averse to fabricating a few of these stories himself. In a letter to Bishop Thomas Savage, dated 21st December 1944, the last sentence of the second paragraph is not the only piece of fiction:

Last week I studied German rule in Poperinghe, and was sickened by the facts which came to me from folk now grown middle-aged, whom Pettifer and I knew as children. Thirty-five men (I think) and two young boys were shot without the slightest form of trial. About a hundred men were taken from their beds long after midnight and sent into Silesian slavery. Homes have not heard of them since they were seized, and wives were told not to enquire after them.

The Old House was a very drunken billet for German Officers who fell down stairs. Our precious relics were fortunately all spirited away by brave townsfolk, buried, preserved and now returned intact. Praise be to God! The House was left in a most swinish state, and only saved by Belgian electricians from being blown up by a scheduled act of demolition on departure.

The Herrenvolk got the wind up after D-Day and scuttled out of Poperinghe one morning, commandeering every cart, bicycle and even pram to carry their loot. So typical of them!

Setting aside these accounts, for almost a week members of the local Belgian resistance forces stood guard over the Old House with the assistance of some R.A.F. personnel temporarily stationed in the vicinity of Poperinghe. By the end of the month permission had been granted, to Paul Slessor and Barclay Baron to return to Poperinghe. On arrival they were feted like celebrities, and it was not long before they were overseeing the replacement of contents, effecting repairs and greeting an ever growing number of British service personnel to the house. During these early days the Friends of Talbot House provided a canteen for almost twenty-four hours a day, brewing gallons of tea, making sandwiches and answering visitors' questions. A British armoured division arrived in Poperinghe, its young soldiers crowding into the House returned the spirit of "Everyman". All that was missing was Tubby, he returned the week commencing 11th December 1944:

... the Beloved House has shaken off this nightmare of oppression and misuse. It stands

**191**

almost immune, and much venerated not only by the British Troops in rest, but by the townsfolk. Many generations will owe to the patience, wit and courage of these RC homes the restitution of the vestry linen, the Sacramental Plate (all in good order and beautifully cleaned), and above all the Carpenter's Bench itself.

I was not in the House for half an hour before a soldier came in out of the night to make his confession. Voluntary Prayers and Preparations for Communion went forward as of old. The Celebrations were (to my faithless surprise) furnished well with joyful guests.

# CHAPTER
# THIRTEEN

# A Day in the Life

Those who return shall find that peace endures,
Find old things old, and know the peace they knew,
Walk in the garden, slumber by the fireside,
Share the peace of dawn, and dream amid the dew.
*Leslie Coulson — Those who return.*

Following the advent of the first organised battlefield tours in the 1920's, and in particular the Toc H and St. Barnabas Pilgrimages of 1923 and 1926, the first visitors to Talbot House were almost exclusively Toc H members or ex-servicemen and their families. After the acquisition of the house in 1929 a more varied clientele began to arrive amongst whom were students and historians of the Great War. At the time Tubby remarked:

The thing which began there, in that big white house, did not end with the war. It moved home and you may gladly come and see it if you will; for Toc H is too much involved in the lives of a vigorous fellowship, some 20,000 strong, to think of singing its Nunc Dimittis. True, the task in the Empire is far more complex than it was in Flanders; but the need is even more urgent, for the Ypres Salient was full at least of unstinted comradeship, but civil life is of the most uncivil kind. In the Salient, too, you were involved in an enterprise so great that you became great to sustain it. In London you work on a high stool at something you despise, and live only when you leave it. Yes, London, Calcutta and Buenos Aires are uglier, lonelier and more dangerous places than Ypres, and the casualties are unnumbered and inglorious.

During the 1930's it was used one evening a month as a meeting place for the War Graves Commission gardeners employed in the area.

This proved popular to these men who, often working in remote cemeteries involving long hours and travel, might not encounter an English speaking person for weeks at a time.

John Burgess, who very nearly met his end whilst in Tubby's employ, spoke of the House as:

The House is an incredible place, it presents people with the opportunity to have a vision, a snap-shot if you like, of what happened; and in particular what happened to the people, because men of rank and no rank came together to accept each other on a first name basis. They went away from here back to being, perhaps, solicitors or bus drivers, but because they were in the community so they were able to give something back to the community;

often in Toc H groups which enabled local Toc H to flourish and grow.

He also related the unusual manner in which Tubby would sometimes "spread the word and enlarge the flock":

He had a great gift for spotting people and giving them the opportunity to do things they wouldn't have done under normal circumstances. Sometimes we would be preparing a meal in his rooms on Tower Hill, and we would be two people short. He would go out and he'd find somebody, and they would be very surprised when they were suddenly confronted by this very small man who would grab them by the arm, drag them in and say "Look, we want you to come to lunch. Tell us what you do." He would find an American tourist or a Billingsgate fish porter and these amazed people would find themselves sitting with an ambassador from New Zealand or somebody; there were always 8 people at lunch and if he was one short he'd simply go out and find someone. They'd be suddenly embraced by this little man who never sat still, never ate a meal, always walked round and round the table talking to everybody, involving everybody, always saying that he was the same height sitting down as standing up, so why should he sit down.

For a short while after the Second World War the number of visitors to Talbot House was comparable to that of the pre-war period, but suddenly, and without apparent reason, their number began to fall. For almost two and a half decades it seemed as if the two world wars had been forgotten. Such was the lack of interest in the Western Front, and so few were the visitors, Toc H and the Association considered selling it. However, after the 60th anniversary celebrations of the Somme and Passchendaele battle in the late 1970's, a dramatic increase of visitors was noted.

Tubby himself was a frequent visitor, often arriving unannounced and the duration of his stay uncertain. He had written of his experiences in *Tales of Talbot House* and *Plain Tales from Flanders* and regularly contributed to the "Toc H Journal". Reflecting on the enterprise of Toc H. begun all those years before in Talbot House:

As I look back tonight on the Old House in Poperinghe where all this work began under God's hand, I find it is impossible to brood on failures and disappointments. I cannot be so blind and ignorant as to neglect, or minimise, the truth that our first fellowship and dedication came through some friends whose bodies now rest in Flanders. Yet, the heart and soul of the Old House still flows like a tide of joy and light, out of the old Upper Room and through the Lamps that are faithfully maintained by men of all conditions and of many races.

On Saturday, 3rd November 1962, one month before his 74th birthday, after 40 years as vicar of All Hallows,

Tubby retired. In 1965 while attending the 50th Anniversary celebrations of the opening of Talbot House he was made a Freeman of Poperinghe, the first person to receive the honour in forty years, and presided over the opening of the newly named street in the town, Toc H Straat, in honour of the association.

He last visited Talbot House in September 1972. He died on 16th December of that year and five days later his ashes were interred in the crypt of All Hallows-by-the-Tower beside those of his two great friends and helpers in his work at Talbot House, Neville Talbot and Arthur Pettifer, His Epitaph, composed by himself, reads:

Lord Jesu, Redeemer,
Wilt wake an old dreamer?
Of workers the weakest,
Of liegemen the least,
Of faint-hearts most faithless,
Of Saints' scars too scatheless —
Wilt robe in Redemption, a fool for thy Feast?

# CHAPTER
# FOURTEEN

# Notices and Daily Orders

The two notice boards in the hallway of the house were both centres of constant activity with the first, "Friendship Corner" constantly surrounded by men adding notes giving or asking for information on friends, family or colleagues, or by men searching for news of the same. The second used by Tubby for "Notices and Daily Orders" informed the visitor on the house activities and rules. This one was a source of entertainment as well as information, as Tubby always chose to communicate in a humourous, friendly and inoffensive manner, no matter whether the subject be of a serious or general nature. He frequently used spelling mistakes to put his point across: *No Swaring Aloud Hear*. Sadly, some of the signs known to have existed in the House have disappeared: *Come into the Garden* is a 1990's reproduction as is the sign at the foot of the stairs: *Come upstairs and risk meeting the padre* — who said:

Our wall-paperdom, therefore, was in its way, half the secret of the drawing power of Talbot House. It was a house proper — not one large bare hall with a counter at one end and a curtain at the other, but a house, like home, with doors and windows and carpets and stairs and many small rooms, none of them locked; so that you never knew whom or what you might find next. Obviously the place belonged to you in a home-like way, and relied on you being kind to it in return. There were pictures in frames, not patriotic prints either; and vases full of cut flowers; and easy chairs; and open fireplaces, with a tabby cat (Duchess) to teach you how to see what you wanted most by blinking into the golden glow.

The following lists some of the messages that survived the war, many now framed and hanging in the hallway and rooms on the ground floor of the house.

## FRIENDSHIP CORNER

Gunner S. Morrison, "D" Howitzer Battery, 21 Bde., R.E.A., B.E.F. would like to hear from Pte. G. Morrison. (An added pencil note by the Gunner's name reads — Killed.)

Sgt. H.N. Copsey, 8056, 2nd Devon Regt., would like to meet his brother P.F. Copsey. (An added pencil note reads — Wounded.)

Gunner R. Villiers, 102058, 217 Siege Battery, R.G.A. (Who presumably wished to hear from anyone who knew him.) (an added pencil note — Died in Action.)

Can No. 312508. Driver James Pike, R.G.A., meet his brother No.38699. Pte. E Pike, 22nd Cheshire Regt.

134758. Sapper Robson, G.T., 130th Field Co., R.E., will see his brother Jack here or if he enquires for the 25th Division, 7th Bde., he will find me. Thompson.

## NOTICES AND DAILY ORDERS

Do not leave cycles outside — they will be scrounged by passers by.

Do not leave cycles in the hall — they will be borrowed by the Chaplain.

You may leave cycles in the garden — there it is hoped they will be safe!

EXCELSIOR.

"The number of otherwise intelligent human beings who hang about the hall, reading silly notices, and catching well deserved colds, is most distressing.

An occasional straggler drags himself up the staircase, generally in futile search for the canteen, which confronts him in the garden.

Otherwise oil and fuel upstairs waste their sweetness, and the rooms and pictures their welcome."

NOTICE.

To all members of the human race and others, who are unwise enough to enter this House.

You are "for it" now. Once inside Talbot House, and there's no saying what you will have to do to get out again. You may of course be in luck's way, and out of mine. Hundreds of men have come in and out several times, and lived to tell the tale of a peaceful hour in an armchair with a neighbours snores for a lullaby. On the other hand, if a middle aged parson in a tennis blazer sights you, it's all up. You will find yourself mending electric bells, tipping cues, mending lamps or licking envelopes, before you know where your support line is. Can you sing; recite; act; conjure; debate; play chess; paint scenery; run a cinema? Even if you can't it won't make any difference. He is always doing things he can't do. If you come from Australia, he was born there. From London: he was educated (!) there. From Hampshire he lives there. He knows seven words of Welsh and has even been to Scotland. The best thing to do is to promise him what he wants, to keep him quiet; and quickly camouflaging yourself with a red hat-band, you will find him flee you. PB.C. (1917)

UNWELCOME VISITORS.

Welcome yourself to Talbot House. We don't put "salve mass" on the doorstep, but have a salvage dump next door to make up for it. But we want you to feel it is true of your arrival just the same. For you are surely not one of those who —

1) Imagine the House has an off-licence for magazines, stationery, etc., e.g., I put a current number of Nash's magazine in a cover, heavily

**201**

stamped, on the first floor last week. In twenty-four hours the cover was empty. This is how misanthropes are made.

2) Imagine we have the Y.M.C.A. or some unlimited funds at our back. At present we are trying hard (like my Sam Browne does) to make two ends meet. Three noble Divisions (55th, 38th and 39th) help us from their funds. But otherwise we are in a bad way. My tie pin was in pawn long ago: and even the House is in Pop.

Writing materials for use in the House cost some £6 a month, so that he who departs with his pockets full of envelopes is guilty of what Mr Punch cells "Teuton Conduck".

3) Woe worth the imbecile who begins three letters one after another on three sheets of paper, with a fourth to try nibs and fancy spelling on; and, with one large boot on a fifth sheet and the other on a pad of blotting-paper, splashes ink about like a cuttle fish (is it?), and draws a picture (libellous, we hope) of "my darling Aggie" on a sixth sheet, and then remembers that he really came in to play billiards.

The House aims at reminding you a little bit of "your ain folk". Hence pictures, flowers and freedom. Help to strengthen the illusion of being a Club-able spirit.

This is not a G.R.O., but just a G.R.O.U.S.E. by the poor old chaplain.

Tubby refers to difficulty with his Sam Browne in the above notice. Dr. Leonard Browne, RAMC, was driven to distraction by Tubby's untidy appearance and wrote:

Clothing was always a trial — buttons "would" persist in coming off, breeches "would" gape at the knees, shirt cuffs "would" wear out — but after all an innkeeper of the highest order has no time to dally with such details of artificial civilisation.

## EXCHANGE AND MART.

A handsome, kindly, and middle aged individual, who prefers to remain anonymous, finds that his neck is growing thicker through long years of warfare, with the result that seventeen-inch shirts and seventeen and a half collars produce a perpetual strangulation. If this should catch the eye of any gentleman upon whose neck the yoke of Army life is producing the contrary effect an exchange of wardrobe would be to the welfare of both.

Address, P.B.C., C.E, The Office, T.H.

## STOP PRESS.

A tidy draft of woollies — i.e., socks, etc. — has reached T.H. from the ever generous Mrs. Fry of Bristol. Applications for the same should be made to the Chaplain. All queues prohibited by Sir A. Yapp. Allotment — one sock per battalion. January 14th, 1918.

On the subject of laundry, Tubby's letter of 23rd May 1918, reads:

I have practically nothing left now that matters. Even of my own clothes, I am only keeping what I stand up in. In point of fact my wardrobe is badly depleted by a bad business a fortnight back, when a shell hit one washerwoman's house and killed her and all her family. All our washing went at the same time — it seems trivial to mention it, but it leaves me short of socks, etc.. But Mrs Fry is sending some. Curiously enough last summer when our washing was done over the road, a small shell spoilt it all, and it had to be redone!

A Sapper assisting Tubby inadvertently took the Padre's penknife and next morning the following was on the notice-board:

NOTICE.

If the Sapper who helped me yesterday, and left his penknife in my room, will apply to me he will receive two apologies -

1. An apology for the trouble I am giving him.

2. The apology for a knife which he left behind. P.B.C.

RATS!

On the principle by which Mrs. Beeton is said to begin her chapter on the cooking of apples with a brief reference to the Fall of Man, this notice should open with some reference to the anti-episcopal tendencies displayed by rats in the lamentable food-hoarding case of the late Bishop Hatto. But our need is too great for literary allusions.

What the House has to face is a plague of rats, all of them heavy or welter-weight, against Don Whiskerandos, our cat, who is feather-weight only, so can't be expected to make good.

Wanted therefore; the loan of a good ratting terrier, ferrets, or other rat-strafing rodent.

A rat seen last night measured about four feet from stem to stern.

OUR ANIMAL KINGDOM.

Have you been formally introduced to — Kitten, one, white, camouflaged. Belge by parentage, but British (as the catechism says) by adoption and grace. It enjoys the war enormously, and is far too busy getting dirty to have time to spare for getting clean. It has a limited but vivacious repertoire of performances and has betrayed several Scotsmen into forgetting themselves so far as to smile.

The Love Birds. Their names "Hunter" and "Bunter" are, as Sam Weller said of the sausage, "wropt in mystery." Hunter is plain in appearance; Bunter is spot. They came from Boulogne in a five ton lorry, and do nothing in particular, but do it very well.

The Jackpie or Magdaw. His name is "Jacko" and his diet "burly beef" and collar studs. He came from a reserve trench at Elverdinghe: we clipped his wings on arrival, since when he flies much better than before. No! we decline to slit his tongue, in the hope that he will talk articulately. He talks Welsh perfectly at present.

## EXTRACTED FROM A.C.G's. INSTRUCTIONS, FIFTH ARMY.

(b) it is objectionable to describe a chaplain as Colonel, Major or Captain, as it tends to obscure the Chaplain's privileged position of priest ministering to all ranks. Each Chaplain should discourage both of ficers and men from addressing him by army rank: compare ruling of Adjutant-General D/3657, 31/3/17. "The badges of rank worn by Chaplains do not carry with them the use of military titles." For your information and necessary action, please. Try and help the Chaplain's work by clearing the air of this miserable delusion.

Tubby added a note to the above:

i.e. the things on our shoulders are only camouflage, and we are really meant, as the King's Regulations in the wise old Royal Navy put it, to be "the friend and advisor of all on board".

# HOW TO FIND YOUR BEARINGS ON A DARK NIGHT WITHOUT A COMPASS. THIS IS AN OLD SCOUT'S TIP.

"Take a watch, not your own, tie a string on to it, swing it round your head three times, and then let go, saying to the owner: "That's gone West."

The points of the compass being thus established, you proceed rapidly in the safest direction."

# THE WASTE PAPER BASKETS ARE PURELY ORNAMENTAL
by Order: P.B.C.

# HOW THE WHEELS GO ROUND. BY I.O.U. CORPS.

For the next few days, the total staff of the House is five, including Jimmy, the presiding magician of the maconachie. A reasonable complement for the House, hall and garden is eleven, including the canteen. So, if the antimacassars aren't watered, or the aspidistras dusted, or the pot-pourri jars distributed for a few days, don't think "there's something rotten in the state of Denmark."

# NOTICE.

Owing to the descent of a meteorite upon the electric lighting plant, the House is temporarily reduced to the oil and grease expedients of a bygone age. In regard to the former, gentlemen will please desist from turning the wick upwards, as the augmentation of the illumination thus secured is extremely temporary, and results in a soot bath and a cracked chimney. In regard to the latter, remember what Shakespeare says about its illuminant attractiveness, and please draw the blinds. October 2nd 1917.

Talbot House also supported The Hannah Mitchell Fund which was continued by Toc H after the war until Hannah began her career. Hannah was the daughter of a King's Own Scottish Borderers' veteran, invalided out of the army in 1916 and who later died of tuberculosis:

For three years the House collected more than the yearly maintenance of an adopted child for the "Waifs and Strays Society". This little girl, whom none of us had ever seen, was the object of the most affectionate solicitude among small and great. The Military Police in the Prison at Ypres collected eagerly on her behalf even during the exceedingly rough period of April, 1917. Major Harry Jago, DSO, MC, of 2nd Devons, asks anxiously for her in the last letter before his death. One Lancashire lad, than whom no more loyal friend could be met with, told me for three Sundays in succession how his officer was giving a prize for the best kept mules. And it was not until one night, when he came in triumph and laid the prize money in my hand for the little girl, that I knew the secret of his ambition. Yet another, having lost his sole chance of leave, through its closing down for the fighting time ahead, paid in the hundred francs that he had saved to spend at home. If any endowment ever carried blessings with it, Hannah Mitchell was blessed indeed.

Three notices on the subject were posted in 1918:

Every Lent Talbot House has collected a considerable sum for the "Waifs and Strays Society". Last year we set ourselves the ambitious task of adopting a child — Hannah Mitchell by name (aged 8) — and paying for her maintenance under the excellent care of the Society. The result was splendid. More than £20 was raised here, and another £2 in the Prison at Ypres. This Lent, the society have asked us to undertake her maintenance for another twelve months. This will mean a big effort, and widespread sympathy and self denial; the vein of copper is more difficult to work than it was last year, and that of silver almost beyond reach. But if every one helps who can, we shall do it. Collecting boxes will be placed in various parts of the House; and may gladly be had for the various messes in the neighbourhood. All Church Collections will go to the same object, until Easter. Already donations of 20 frs (HAC) and 1 fr (Sigs) have come in, before this notice is posted."

Remember: "What I spent, I lost: What I gave, I have." 14.2.18. PBC.

HANNAH MITCHELL FUND.

I am getting rather windy as to the £18, which is our minimum endowment required for our "Waifs and Strays Society" contribution, in order that the House may not fail this year for the first time to support our adopted child. We have about £10 so far, with only another fortnight to go. Of course, there are several boxes out which will help greatly if they come back in the same plethoric condition in which they returned recently from the Wheeler-Sergeant of the Essex Battery. But there will have to be real generosity during the next fortnight if we are to make good. Meanwhile, may I thank Pte. Wallace, who does not give his address, for the gift of 10 frs, which is going to the fund. All Sunday offertories, etc., also go to it, until Easter Day. 18.3.18. P.B. Clayton.

Hannah Mitchell is safely provided for during another year. The Old House has raised in all £16. 1s. 8d, to which Little Toc H is adding another £6, raised in Wipers, also during Lent.

For the information of the casual visitor it must be explained that the child is the adopted daughter of Talbot House, which guarantees to pay £22 per annum for her maintenance to the "Waifs and Strays Society". This year, owing to local conditions of change and depletion, the task looked well nigh beyond our reasonable hopes, but thanks to the real sacrifice of several true Talbotousians, it is faithfully accomplished. Laus Deo. 2.4.18. P.B. Clayton.

Meanwhile it is also a joy to announce that the Easter Offertory for the Army Ordination Candidates Fund totalled the magnificent sum of 250 francs, and this with the town practically deserted. PBC.

Following the order for closure on 14th April and it's subsequent reprieve, Tubby posted the following information for visitors:

## T.H. AND THE RECENT GALE OF WIND.

When the history of the House is written, the last fortnight will have a paragraph to itself. Until a fortnight ago, the grand Old House was apparently resigned to a placid old age in the suburbs of war, where the rumours germinate. Suddenly at 11.30p.m. on Sat. week, came a bolt from the blue, a pink order saying "Shut up." To this we replied sleepily: "shut up yourself." Sunday brought the same refrain: "shut up," to which we replied "shut up?" Monday put the lid on it. Our staff was withdrawn, and we reported broken-heartedly "shut up!" Meanwhile on Sunday night the staff of Little Toc H in Wipers was given sudden notice to quit. On Monday Mr Goodwin led a sortie and got away the piano, etc. (we had only put the last nail in our new concert hall there twenty four hours previously!). On Tuesday, enters the hero of the piece in the person of APM Pop. He championed our cause to such effect, that my movement order is cancelled, and the House is left, denuded, it is true, of staff and creature comforts, but "semper eadem" (I forgot the Latin dictionary is at present in pawn with our noble friends of ROD). We hope soon to have the House in apple pie order again; meanwhile you will only drive us to misanthropy if you persist in strewing nutshells on the floor. 22.4.18. PBC.

When the House re-opened, within the hour the following two notices appeared on the board:

October 1st: "Pheasant shooting begins and Charles Letts' Diaries for 1919 are published." Hitherto the world has apparently no memorable event to which the day is sacred. Future generations will however remember it as the day on which Poperinghe re-opened, and Talbot House was found, like Macbeth's Scotland, standing where it stood.

Since you saw it last, the mice have broken all the windows, aerated the concert hall — which was always stuffy — and punctured the roof and garden wall in several places. But good fairies have been busy since then, and the paint and white-wash are scarcely dry.

You will find some alterations, which we hope you will approve; but the Dramatis Personae remain much the same —

e.g. Chief of Staff — Eddie Evans, the Welsh Comedian.

George, the Librarian — L/Cpl. G. Trower.

The Man that knocks the hammer with the nails — A. Rose.

First Aid — C. Vokins.

The Strong Man from Ireland — P. Flynn.

The General — A. Pettifer.

Actor-Manager — C.Wilmott, and so forth.

The first floor is ready for you, with a larger Library and a bigger billiard table. PBC.

TALBOT HOUSE, 35, Rue de l'Hopital — 200 yards from the Square.

The dear old House is now open again, like the flowers in May. Like them, its first attempt at opening met with a cold snap so it went to sleep again. Now the lawful time for awakening has come, and it proceeds with prudence to unfold itself. The ground floor is pretty well advanced.The first floor is partially ready.The second floor is totally bare still.The Chapel in the attic (the oldest chapel in the BEF) is practically complete again; and services will be held on Sunday at the old times, DV.

On the day of our opening, four of the Staff have gone on leave, long overdue. So the blue blazer will be dirtier than ever during the next fortnight.

Owing to the canteen shortage, the Church Army are helping us by running a tea-room in the Nissen hut dans le jardin, but you will have to wait for your grocery queue till the CA canteen opens in the Square, etc. Mr Legge, a fellow citizen of "Pompey" with myself, is the Church Army worker who is kindly taking the tea and biscuit problem off my rheumatic old shoulders; so that all epicures, who do (or don't) like Sergeant-Major's tea, will find themselves up against him, while I hold the sponge and the prize money.

213

P.S. — The absence of a canteen will mean to the House the loss of its only certain source of income. So presents of books, etc., for the Library will not only win a smile from George, but will provide what we can no longer afford to buy. My wristwatch was in pawn long ago; and even the House is in Pop. 1.10.18 PBC.

As the tide of war flowed rapidly towards the Rhine, Poperinghe and Talbot House were left far behind. The Salient was now inhabited almost exclusively by Labour Battalions involved in "sanitising" the battlefields. The steady flow of visitors to the Old House became no more than a trickle; prompting this notice of 20th October:

TO MOVE OR NOT TO MOVE, THAT IS
THE QUESTION.

Owing to the inconsiderate retirement of our old neighbour, the Boche, Toc H is in a pretty fix. If we move — e.g. to Courtrai — we may be high and dry by the time we have reached it with all our lorry loads of belongings. Also if the period of demobilisation is really at hand, this may be an important salvage centre. And once we vacate the House, we shall never get in again. Briefly, therefore, TH will remain here for the present.

For if the Boche goes to Brussels, we shan't cut any ice in Courtrai.

Or if the Boche goes to Blazes, we shall be wanted here QED.

214

But we expect you to get down here somehow, and see us sometimes.You really must try.

When Tubby returned from his travels over the Armistice period he found a note from Neville Talbot dated 11th November 1918:

"DEAREST TUB,
I am glad. Fitch is lovely. I have written a line. O that you were with me or rather I with you for this new wonderful period. I made a forlorn hope (to) ask for you when I met DCG and Andy today together. But it was met with MG fire. But I am glad about your news -and it's all one front and one cause and one King.

Darling Dick — but for you, my great pal out here. Let me share in any brain or rather soul waves.

How miraculous the hour "Thy righteousness standeth like the strong mountains, Thy judgements are like the great deep".

Ever with love, NST."

On the reverse of the above Tubby added:

This characteristic note from Neville Talbot was written on the first Armistice Day. Fitch was my new DACG, 19th Corps. Andy was Rev. F.I.

**215**

Anderson, ACG, 2nd Army. Dick was Dick Dugdale, killed in the last advance.

NOTICE.

In honour of the return of Paddy (Pte. Flynn) from leave to his post on the staff of the House, the following chestnut is issued to all concerned:

SCENE: Irish parade-ground.

DRILL SERGEANT: "Now then, Rafferty, get those big feet of yours in line, can't you!"

PTE. RAFFERTY: "Arrah! Sergeant, they're no my feet at all, at all. They're Pte. Murphy's in the back row".

Mid-October 1918.

The following two notices, were among the last to appear.

VICTORY — AND AFTER.

For three and a half years Britain (and the world in general) has been trying to turn citizens into good soldiers.The time is coming when we must start turning soldiers into good citizens.The task is going to be a tremendous one, and must begin, at latest, now. In Talbot House we mean to do our bit of study and self-education.
On Tuesday mornings at 11a.m. papers will be read by experts on, e.g.
Town Planning
Municipality as Landlord

Public Health, etc.

A popular discussion on the same lines will be held on Wednesday evenings.

On Thursdays, 4.30–6.15p.m., similar discussions, e.g. on "education", will be held in the Chaplain's Room, to which all are welcome.

The Library now has a special section dealing with Social Problems. 2.12.18. PBC

FIXTURES FOR THIS WEEK.

Tuesday, 11.30a.m., in the Chaplain's Room. An Officer's meeting to discuss a paper by Lieut. Redfern on: — Town Planning and Housing.

Wednesday, 7.00p.m.,The same lecture in the Hall at a general meeting, followed by questions.

Thursday, 4.30p.m., in the Chaplain's Room. A conference on "Moral Education".

6.45p.m., A Chess Tournament in the Hall, at which the challenger will play twelve games simultaneously.

Saturday, 7.00p.m., A Dramatic Performance by the Talbot House Party.

Of all the sermons given by Tubby in the Upper Room of Talbot House, only one was preserved for posterity. Appropriately it is the last delivered by him in the Chapel. Dated the 21st Sunday after Trinity (27th October 1918) its theme "The Hope Of Immortality", it closed:

Go thy way, thy son liveth. — St. John IV.50.

So, tonight, here in this old chapel, the spiritual centre for three years of the old salient now finally freed, between us and those who have freed it there lies that great belt of desolation that we know only too well. It is hideous still, but full of fear no longer; for those who have at last broken the ring of death are far beyond it now: out of our sight, because victorious; vanished, because advancing. Desolation, it is true, divides us but neither we nor they are desolate. We go on our way here for the time, happy for the knowledge that their feet, as they go forward, are on ever firmer ground. P.B. Cl.

## SPECIAL ORDERS NO. 1 SECTION. 13/3/18

1) This position will be held, and the Section will remain here until relieved.

2) The enemy cannot be allowed to interfere with the programme.

3) If the Section cannot remain here alive, it will remain here dead, but in any case it will remain here.

4) Should any man through shell shock or other case attempt to surrender, he will remain here dead.

5) Should any guns be blown out, the Section will use Mills Grenades and other novelties.

6) Finally the position as stated will be held.

E.P. Bethune, Lieut., C/C., No. 1 Section.

The story of this order is little known outside of Australia. Towards the end of February 1918 the 3rd Machine Gun Company, A.I.F., was moving into the line and two officers were sent forward to reconnoitre the position where forward machine-guns were to be posted. They reported to Lieutenant Bethune that the position was hopeless as it had a field of fire of no more than six yards. If the enemy attacked the crews would be killed before they could fire a shot. Lieutenant Bethune protested to his C.O. but to no avail, so Bethune insisted as a matter of honour on being the officer in charge of the post. He called for volunteers, and every man of his section stepped forward. He selected three veterans and three new men.

As Bethune led his men to the position he was overtaken by a runner who told him that orders had changed; he was to take up positions at Buff Bank. This was much more to the young officer's liking. He positioned his gun teams, loaded all spare belts and placed 10,000 rounds per gun ready to hand.

With the safety of that part of the front entirely in his hands, Lieutenant Bethune considered it only right that each man should have written orders. "I wanted to make it absolutely clear to the men exactly what our job was," Bethune said in 1937, "so that if a man had to die, he should die in his own light-hearted fashion, in goodly company."

The position was held and the crew survived, though some of the men were later killed. Bethune's battle order was circulated by H.Q.1 Div., A.I.F., and later by other staffs. In the American forces copies were

219

mimeographed and distributed as "an admirable model of all that a set of standing trench orders should be".

It should be emphasised that Lieutenant Bethune did not seriously believe that his men might surrender. He himself said, "They knew that I knew that they could not consider such a possibility and so between us we enjoyed in silence the joke that to an outsider might have seemed a little grim. My name is connected with the orders that I wrote but it was the fighting men beside me who made the words come, for this was the spirit in which they fought throughout those years and I only translated into words the spirit of the fighting A.I.F."

Unsolicited Testimonials from Public Figures

THE KAISER WIRELESSES: As our good old German Shakespeare says, in the "Merchant of Vienna" (sic!) "A plague on both your Houses."

HILAIRE BELLOC REMARKS, in his monumental work "The War Hour by Hour, from every Possible and Impossible, Human and Inhuman Standpoint." (Vol.666, p.999):- "The psychological reasons which led to our long tenure of the Salient are now increasingly apparent to all soldiers; they were not merely international, but 'highly domestic'."

HENRY V (per the late Lewis Waller) DECLAIMS: "Talbot ... shall be in their flowing cups freshly remembered."

LORD NORTHCLIFFE DICTATES: "Whatever sinister influences may operate at home, patriotic ardour is, as ever, the temper of our vast Armies. So eager are our gallant men to meet the foe, that I myself have seen great queues of men formed up in communication trenches, unable to find room in the front line.The fierce light of Mars gleams in every eye.Thus it has been found necessary to establish counter-attacks behind the lines. Some of these places, one in particular, are almost as redolent of luxury as Donnington Hall itself."

HORATIO BOTTOMLEY SPEAKS OUT: When I left the shell-swept area of General Headquarters, the dull reverberation of machine-guns made me, like an old soldier, wrap my gas helmet closer round my knees. Haig — you may trust him — I say, you may trust him — said to me: "Keep your napper down, old man; think what your life means to England."

On our way back, we motored through a small town, which the General beside me especially asked me not to specify to my two million readers. We flashed past the gloomy doorway of a miserable House in a narrow street. A smug and sour faced parson stood in the doorway of the so called Soldier's Club, with a bundle of tracts in one hand and a subscription list in the other. Mark my words. You know the type. The so called Church has not stirred a finger anywhere in the war zone for anyone.

# GLOSSARY

| | |
|---|---|
| AA | Assistant. |
| aaa | Signallers parlance to separate sentences within a message. |
| ACG | Army Chaplain General. |
| ADC | Aide De Camp. |
| Adjt | Adjutant. |
| ADMS | Assistant Director of Medical Services. |
| AGM | Annual General Meeting. |
| AIF | Australian Imperial Force. |
| APM | Assistant (or Area) Provost Marshall. |
| APO | Army Post Office. |
| ASC | Army Service Corps. |
| ASHdrs | Argyll & Sutherland Highlanders. |
| AT | Army Transport. |
| Attd | Attached. |
| AVC | Army Veterinary Corps. |
| Battn | Battalion (also abbreviated to Bn.). |
| BEF | British Expeditionary Force. |
| Bde | Brigade (also abbreviated to Brig.). |
| B'ty | Battery. |
| Capt | Captain. |
| CASC | Canadian Army Service Corps. |
| CCS | Casualty Clearing Station. |
| CEF | Canadian Expeditionary Force. |
| CEMS | Church Ecumenical Mens' Society. |
| C of E | Church of England. |
| CF | Chaplain's Force. |
| CG | Coldstream Guard. |
| C in C | Commander in Chief. |

| | |
|---|---|
| Cmdg | Commanding. |
| Col | Colonel. |
| CO | Commanding Officer. |
| Coy | Company. |
| DCG | Deputy Chaplain General. |
| DCLI | Duke of Cornwall's Light Infantry. |
| DSO | Distinguished Service Order. |
| Divn | Division (also abbreviated to Div.). |
| EFC | Expeditionary Forces Canteen. |
| FAU | Friends Ambulance Unit. |
| GHQ | General Headquarers. |
| GRO | General Routine Order. |
| GRU | Graves Registrati on Unit. |
| HAC | Honourable Artillery Company. |
| IB | Infantry Brigade. |
| IWGC | Imperial War Graves Commission. |
| IWM | Imperial War Museum. |
| KOSB | King's Own Scottish Border Regt. |
| KOYLI | King's Own Yorkshire Light Infantry. |
| KRRC | King's Royal Rifle Corps. |
| KSLI | King's Shropshire Light Infantry. |
| Laus Deo | Praise God (Latin). |
| Liber Vitae | Book of Life (Latin). |
| Lt. | Lieutenant. |
| Lt. Col. | Lieutenant Colonel. |
| MC | Military Cross. |
| MFP | Military Foot Police. |
| MGC | Machine Gun Corps. |
| MM | Military Medal. |
| MO | Medical Officer. |
| MT | Motor Transport. |

| | |
|---|---|
| NCO | Non-Commissioned Officer. |
| Nisi Dominus Frustra | We Achieve Nothing Without Divine Assistance |
| Nunc Dimittis | Now (Into Thy Hands O Lord) I entrust (My Spirit). From the book of Common Prayer. |
| Obus | Artillery shells. |
| OR | Other Ranks. |
| OTC | Officer Training Corps. |
| PBC | Philip Byard "Tubby" Clayton. |
| PH | Phenol Helmet (early of Gas Helmet). |
| PM | Provost Marshall. |
| Pte | Private soldier. |
| PTSD | Post Traumatic Stress Syndrome. |
| Q | Quartermaster. |
| QED | Quod Erat Demonstrandum (Latin) "Which was shown/proved". |
| QMS | Quartermaster Sergeant. |
| QWR | Queen's Westminster Rifles. |
| Resurget Domus Talbotensis | May the House of Talbot live again (Latin) |
| RAChD | Royal Army Chaplain's Department. |
| RAF | Royal Air Force. |
| RAMC | Royal Army Medical Corps. |
| RB | Rifle Brigade. |
| RC | Roman Catholic. |
| RE | Royal Engineers. |
| RFA | Royal Field Artillery. |
| RFC | Royal Flying Corps. |

| | |
|---|---|
| RGA | Royal Garrison Artillery. |
| RN | Royal Navy. |
| ROD | Railway Operations Dept. |
| RSM | Regimental Sergeant Major. |
| RTO | Railway Transport Officer. |
| Sapper | Royal Engineer. |
| SCF | Senior Chaplain's Force. |
| Semper Eadem | Always the same, steadfast, loyal, faithful (Latin). |
| Sigs | Signallers or Royal Corps of Signals. |
| SOS | International Distress Signal. |
| Spl | Special. |
| Sqdn | Squadron. |
| SRD | Special Rations Dept. |
| SSAFA | Soldiers', Sailors' and Airman's Families Association. |
| TD | Territorial Decoration. |
| TAB | Typhoid, paratyphoid A and paratyphoid B vaccine. |
| VAD | Voluntary Aid Detachment. |
| VC | Victoria Cross. |
| Wipers | Ypres (Ieper). |
| WWI | World War One. |
| WWII | World War Two. |
| YG | Young Gentlemen; priesthood students of Dean's Yard, Westminster. |
| YMCA | Young Mens' Christian Association. |

# INDEX

**ISIS** publish a wide range of books in large print, from fiction to biography. Any suggestions for books you would like to see in large print or audio are always welcome. Please send to the Editorial department at:

**ISIS Publishing Ltd.**
7 Centremead
Osney Mead
Oxford OX2 0ES
(01865) 250 333

A full list of titles is available free of charge from:
**Ulverscroft large print books**

**(UK)**
The Green
Bradgate Road, Anstey
Leicester LE7 7FU
Tel: (0116) 236 4325

**(Australia)**
P.O Box 953
Crows Nest
NSW 1585
Tel: (02) 9436 2622

**(USA)**
1881 Ridge Road
P.O Box 1230, West Seneca,
N.Y. 14224-1230
Tel: (716) 674 4270

**(Canada)**
P.O Box 80038
Burlington
Ontario L7L 6B1
Tel: (905) 637 8734

**(New Zealand)**
P.O Box 456
Feilding
Tel: (06) 323 6828

Details of **ISIS** complete and unabridged audio books are also available from these offices. Alternatively, contact your local library for details of their collection of **ISIS** large print and unabridged audio books.